Midland
Ghosts & Hauntings

by Anne Bradford & Barrie Roberts

Reports of ghosts, mysterious apparitions, strange
meetings and unexplained events by people across
the Midlands, from Ironbridge to Stratford upon
Avon, Stoke on Trent to Worcester.

****

Quercus
John Roberts
8 Hillside Close, Bartley Green
Birmingham B32 4LT
****

Midland Ghosts & Hauntings
by Anne Bradford & Barrie Roberts

ISBN 1 898136 05 X

First Published 1994

*QuercuS

... publishing interesting books ...

Quercus publishes books about Wales and the Midlands.
We are interested in trees and landscapes, history, battles,
lords and kings, castles and churches, meadows and flowers,
bridges and tunnels. In fact we are interested in anything
that you find interesting.

Currently in print are *Midland Castles*, *The Trackway of the
Cross*, *Sketches of Hales Owen* and *Midland Woods & Forests*.

Future titles include *Midlands Parks*, *Midland Rivers &
Streams*, *Midland Lakes & Ponds*, *Midland Country Houses*
and *Australian Williams*.

We are always interested in ideas and proposals for new titles
If you have an idea but do not think you are up to writing
about it, talk to us anyway. We might suggest coauthorship
with you providing the research.

**8 Hillside Close, Bartley Green, Birmingham
B32 4LT   021 550 3158
(send SAE for further details of books in print)**

WALKWAYS

DaywalkS Footpath Networks

Chaddesley Woods
Clent & Lickey Hills
Cannock Chase
Vale of Llangollen
Wyre Forest

The first two are currently in folded A2
sheet format, sold in a plastic cover.

✱
Strolls & Walks

From each of about twenty places there is a
stroll of a mile of so and a walk of 4 to 6 miles.

Strolls & Walks from Picnic Places (Midlands)
Strolls & Walks from Cotswold Villages
Strolls & Walks from Midland Villages (1995)

✱
Long Distance Routes

Step by step guides in both directions which
often connect with each other and Long Distance
Footpaths. (A2 sheets folded to A5,
but Heart of England Way is a book.)

Llangollen to Bala   Bala to Snowdon
Birmingham to Ludlow   Ludlow to Rhayader
Rhayader to Aberystwyth
Birmingham to Church Stretton
Heart of England Way

8 Hillside Close, Bartley Green, Birmingham B32 4LT
(Send sae for current list & prices.)

The Authors

ANNE BRADFORD published her first book of ghost stories in July 1992. She is well qualified to collect anecdotes from the Midlands, having lived in Hockley, Ladywood, Edgbaston, The Malverns, West Hagley, Handsworth, Smethwick and Studley, eventually settling in Redditch. She had her first article published at the age of eight in the Smethwick Telephone and has dabbled in freelance journalism ever since. She was a mature student at Shenstone Teacher Training College, is married to a Graphic Designer and has three children, all of whom have flown the nest.

BARRIE ROBERTS is a Legal Consultant, specialising in the analysis of evidence. For more than five years he has taught a unique course in Birmingham on Ghosts and Unsolved Mysteries and he is about to start a two year course on the death of John Kennedy. He is the author of *Sherlock Holmes and the Railway Maniac* and the forthcoming *Sherlock Holmes and the Glastonbury Fragment*.

Anne compiled and researched the stories. She wrote to local newspapers asking for readers to send details of their paranoral experiences, interviewed many people and collated all the material into a manuscript.

Barrie analysed the stories in the light of his knowledge of the paranormal. He commented on a selection, sometimes extensively, then wrote the introduction and conclusions.

Contents

(vii)

Introduction and Acknowledgments

Paranormal events, like religion and love, are amongst the most common and absorbing human experiences. Given their mysterious importance to most of us, this book was to be more than just a collection of tales already told and old myths, and not just a lot of spooky stories. We wanted new material, preferably recent reports from living witnesses, and with them should go some analysis and an attempt to make sense of the inexplicable.

We gleaned new material by appeals in local newspapers throughout the Midlands, and the response was impressive. Many thanks to these papers, and to the readers who took the trouble to telephone or write with their stories. We are sorry that we could not publish every contribution but, particularly with premonitions and psychic odours, we had to select a representative few.

Selection was both essential and very difficult. However we gave preference to recent events not previously published, to eye witness accounts from living witnesses and to events which could not easily be attributed to natural causes. Even then, we had too much material for a single book, and so selected one report if we had several from the same area. In the end we still had a substantial book and enough material left over to form a fair part of another.

We do not want to discard these stories but would require some new ones to make a second book. Read this book, and if you or someone you know has had an experience that you think would be interesting to readers, please write to Quercus.

Almost a hundred newspapers were asked to publish a letter asking readers for their paranormal experiences. We do not know how many letters were actually printed but replies came through the following papers.

Berrows Worcester Journal, Bromsgrove Messenger,
Evesham and North Gloucester Admag, Kidderminster Shuttle,
Leamington Observer, Leamington Spa Courier,
Nuneaton Herald and Post, Redditch Observer,
Redditch Advertiser, Solihull News, Stafford Post,
Stourbridge News, Sutton Coldfield Observer,
Walsall Advertiser, Weekend Tribune

Some contributors and journalists were particularly helpful, supplying us with local legends and names of friends who could help. Among these were Eric Hall, Bob Goodall, Martyn Brookes, Ron Miles, Sharon Course (Leamington Observer), Georgina Armstrong, Alys Whiting, and others who do not wish their names to be mentioned.

Background material was provided, in the main, by librarians at the following libraries: Birmingham, Bromsgrove, Coventry, Evesham, Lichfield, Malvern, Redditch, Smethwick, Solihull, Stafford, Warwick, Wolverhampton, Worcester, Wythall.

Our thanks to these sympathetic officials, especially Chris Lattimer, Archivist of Walsall Library and Philippa Hands, the Local History Librarian of Perry Common Library.

The following newspapers gave us permission to reproduce original articles:

Berrows Worcester Journal, Bromsgrove Messenger,
Coventry Evening Telegraph, Redditch Advertiser.

The following authors have kindly given permission for stories to be taken from their books (listed in the Bibliography): Aubrey Gwinnett, Rosalind Prince.

Wolverhampton University supplied most of the information on the haunting of Cosford Aerospace Museum.

A name which is marked with an asterisk shows the contributor did not wish his/her real name to be used.

"There are no such things as Ghosts"

The British Isles are said to be the most haunted territory in the world. Our folklore is replete with supernatural creatures - fairies, elves, headless horsemen, banshees, black dogs, phantom nuns, grey ladies, ghostly monks, and phantom armies. These traditional themes have been joined by phantom omnibuses, headless motorcyclists and ghosts that haunt factories and council houses. Our popular literature revels in the field; Victorian British writers defined the classic ghost story for the rest of the world.

Yet we seem to know as little about the nature of these manifestations as our prehistoric forefathers. It is not surprising that they conceived the idea that something about a human being is not destroyed at death. Living close to nature, hunting their fellow creatures for sustenance, deeply dependent on the world around them, they were acute observers of the ways in which nature worked.

They saw the sun dwindle and die each midwinter, to be born again, and they marked its re-birth in megalithic monuments and celebrated it. They saw ice turned to water and steam; they saw burning wood turned to ashes and smoke; they saw plants spring up in places where they had died away months before. They soon discovered one of nature's fundamental laws - that nothing is destroyed, only changed. Little wonder they evolved a belief that even humans are not destroyed, that at their physical end they survive in some altered form.

At New Grange in Ireland stands a massive megalithic tomb, the oldest building in Europe. Above its entrance arch-aelogists found a horizontal slot, like a letter box. Its purpose eluded them until they recalled a local legend that the midsummer sun shone into the grave. It does not, but the re-born sun of midwinter strikes through that slot at dawn and, for a few minutes, its strengthening beam creeps along the ancient passageway until it lights the chamber where the bones of the dead lay. What is that but a call to the sun to waken the dead as the sun itself has been reborn?

Unable to explain so many things, ancient people attributed events to the spirits of the dead and to spirits of non humans, to trees and rocks, to springs and hills, until all of their real world was paralleled by a half hidden world of supernatural creatures and forces. In these beliefs are rooted our folklore and superstitions.

Our ancient forefathers lived short, desperate lives, filled with danger, pain and disease. Death was ever present and all powerful. They came to believe that the powers of death and darkness could enter the real world through any crack, at any point in time or place where two things joined. Where the sea joined the land, where the night joined the day, where the sun turned at midwinter and midsummer, were points to be protected against the spirits. The coming of Christianity scarcely changed these beliefs, for the new faith also believed in an after life and evil spirits. Samhain, the festival that protected the beginning of winter against evil, became All Hallows, midsummer's eve became Saint John's Eve. We still practice ancient superstitions at Halloween, and well into this century fires burned in Scotland and Ireland to keep away evil at midsummer.

We have inherited thousands of years of belief that the dead live again in some shape and that there are evil spirits trying break into our world. These are the roots of our traditional beliefs in ghosts and demons, and this system of belief worked perfectly well until the enquiring scientific mind began to "explain" the world. So now we know how flowers regenerate, how substances change their nature, what causes lightning. However science still has two large blanks to fill - it has not proved whether or not there is a continuation of life after death of the body, and it has not explained ghosts.

At this juncture the sceptic may throw down this book in disgust and say, "There are no such things as ghosts. Why should science waste its precious time on them?" Read on, and find out that there are. Ordinary people see them every day. The evidence is overwhelming.

This collection is of mainly contemporary ghost stories from one area of Britain, but it makes our point. Here are sad ghosts and happy ghosts, stranger ghosts and recognised ghosts, ghosts that are seen, heard, or sometimes only smelt, frightening ghosts and friendly ghosts; there are haunted mansions, and council houses, fire stations, inns and private houses, schools and factories, even a telephone box.

The geographical area covered in this book contains about ten per cent of Britain's population and embraces many kinds of environment, from the deep countryside to crowded towns. There is one way in which our collection is unbalanced. We had to select from the stories sent to us and many of those left out were stories that we found ordinary, less dramatic or curious than the ones we selected. Perhaps by their very ordinariness they establish hauntings and ghost experiences as frequent, almost commonplace, experiences.

That is the simple reason why science should concern itself with ghosts - because all manner of people experience them in all manner of circumstances. The business of science is to tell us how our world operates. So far it has failed to explain a range of phenomena which have been common since before history. By labelling them ghosts scientists perhaps believe they absolve themselves of the need to examine and explain, leaving that to the huckster and the charlatan.

Most scientists, of course, are paid by governments or commercial firms and will not get bonuses or promotion for investigating the paranormal. Governments only play with it in wartime, witness the US Army's World War II experiments with hypnotising people to kill, the US Navy's experiments with telepathy in 1953 and the highly successful Soviet experiments with transmission of code by telepathy. In peacetime it's back to plain old physics and chemistry.

It is notorious that we have no remedy for the common cold because there is more money to be made selling remedies for the symptoms. BT, Mercury and Ma Bell are not going to be delighted if someone discovers how to make everyone fully telepathic in one easy lesson.

There are some academic scientists who try to address the paranormal. Some of them are quoted in this book, including the Psychology Department of Wolverhampton University. Full marks to them and their American colleagues who have proved (yet again) that humans can communicate at a distance and that some seem able to influence the behaviour of machines, but there are still too few. Only one British University (Edinburgh) has a Chair of Parapsychcology. The present incumbent announced when he took the post that he did not belive in the paranormal and would devote his efforts to proving his point. If the dead do know what is going on in this world, Arthur Koestler who endowed the chair must be spinning in his grave. Come back and haunt him, Arthur.

Charles Hoy Fort was an American who collected accounts of events which seemed to break natural rules as laid down by scientists. In four very funny books, *The Book of the Damned* 1919, *New Lands* 1923, *Lo!* 1931 and *Wild Talents* 1932, he paraded thousands of items of anomalous phenomena, along with many desperately silly explanations offered by scientists. He started from the proposition that a fact which science cannot explain is "damned". His work is continued internationally through INFO - the International Fortean Organisation, and in Britain through the magazine Fortean Times, but most of his facts are still "damned" by scientists - UFO's, sea monsters, spontaneous combustion, falls of living creatures from the sky, ghosts - ghosts are especially damnable.

So we who want to know how things happen are left in no man's land, between self evidently silly explanations or curt dismissals by scientists and the preposterous whimsies of cranks and charlatans, swept along by gullibility and superstition. If we accept the evidence we have precious little sensible help interpreting it. We must pick our own careful, stumbling way.

The common label creates difficulties. When we see an apparition of a friend, and that friend later proves to have died at that time, we call this a ghost. When we experience a vision of a battle that took place years before, we call its participants ghosts as well, yet they are almost certainly not the same thing.

Telepathy, the ability of one person to transmit ideas and images to another at a distance, has been proved time and time again in the laboratory, though its mechanism remains unknown. It provides a ready explanation of the deathbed apparition. It is not surprising that the dying should seek to communicate with distant loved ones, nor that telepathy should allow them to succeed, but the same explanation cannot be applied to battlefield visions. Why should a stranger, unconnected with the event, see and hear a complex re-enactment of past scenes? Calling both phen-omena ghosts confuses any attempt to unravel them.

Many different things shelter behind the label ghost. Some may be complex hallucinations depending on a combination of personality and circumstances; some may be natural phenomena not yet defined; some might be forms of telepathy; others may derive from patterns of energy we do not understand. What seems most unlikely is that one unified theory will ever explain all ghosts. They are too diverse in forms, behaviour and characteristics.

Perhaps we should comment on that oldest of explanations - that ghosts are the returned spirits of the dead. There is precious little evidence for the proposition. While ghosts may appear in the likeness of the dead, they do not behave as complete personalities. Their actions (and occasionally words) are limited and often trivial or nonsensical. They do not suggest that they are a manifestation of the core of a human being, only a pale shadow or a poor recording.

As to those traditional ghosts that are supposed to revisit the dungeons where they suffered torment or execution, it is difficult to imagine why they should. The cellars of the Three Tuns public house in Sutton Coldfield are reputed to be haunted by the ghost of a Cavalier youth who was stoned in the pillory on the nearby green and died in the cellars when the pub was a command post for the Parliamentary army. Why should his spirit return from wherever it went to revisit the place where it was most distressed on earth? What kind of after life imposes such a harrowing duty?

We are not entering the discussion as to whether there is an after life, or what form it may take. That is a matter for faith or science. We merely say that, if science one day provides proof of an after life, this is most unlikely to provide an explanation for all ghosts, if any.

Here and there among the stories we have put our views, other peoples' theories, and attempts at explanations. You can judge the evidence for yourself and ignore or reject them. Yes, people invent sensational stories to attract attention. Yes, witnesses often do not understand what they have seen, do not recall it properly and filter their recall through aspects of their personalities. Even so, there are witnesses in plenty, and you must decide for yourselves if every one of them is fraudulent or mistaken. If even one of them is not, then there is evidence of something that breaks the laws of nature as we understand them. We should enquire further until we discover by what laws these phenomena operate.

Summary of
Questions & Comments

To comment and attempt explanation of each ghost story would
be impossible. Many anecdotes are completely inexplicable and
others, such as those which could be caused by telepathy or
poltergeist activity, often have many similarities. Comments
appear after the most appropriate anecdote, and some of the
questions they address are listed below. The reader may wish
to refer to them when looking at other incidents.

*Do ghosts exist? What are ghosts? Why do women see more
ghosts than men? Can a phenomenon be created?* ("There are no
such things as Ghosts", The Ghosts of Dudley Castle, What are
Ghosts?)

What do I do if the place where I live or work is haunted?
(The House over the Waters, You Too Could Have a Ghost)

*Is the human personality (or soul or psyche) capable of
communicating with itself across the ordinary time stream?*
(Simon Returns)

*Is the Vanishing Hitch-hiker deeply embedded in our
subconscious?* (The Vanishing Hitch-hiker)

*How can major events, such as battles, undergo ghostly re-
enactment? Is the ghostly white horse of Edgehill Prince
Rupert's charger or the Horse of Tysoe?* (The Phantom
Battle) *What about minor events?* (The Scouts of Clayhanger
Lane)

*Can telepathic images be transmitted into the dreams of
sleepers?* (Grandad's House)

*What possible explanation could there be for a young man
being confronted by a spirit?* (A Pillar of Mist, The Settee)

Can animals be ghosts? (The Phantom Battle, Jumping Sam, The Phantom Cat)

Can ghosts be telepathic images? Can telepathic images be enhanced by dull, monotonous routines? What are out of body phenomena? (The Real Betty Bates, The Settee)

Why do building operations sometimes seem to disturb ghosts? (Mrs Popoff, The Haunted Shopping Centre)

Would a circle or a pentagram found on the floor of a house explain the paranormal phenomena? (Out of the Circle)

Are you more psychically alert in a state of stress? (Receiving the Past)

What, or who, is a Banshee? (The Banshee)

Can ghosts touch people? (A Pillar of Mist, The Haunted Fire Station, Jumping Sam, Out of the Circle, Miss Morris, The Amorous Ghost, The House over the Waters)

Of what significance is the Ouija Board? ("Because we love it here.", Colin & the Oiuja Board)

What is a poltergeist? Can poltergeist activity be continued after death and can it occur in adults? (Miss Morris, Little Charlie)

Do children see more ghosts than adults? Why do ghosts behave in a silly way? (The Children's Secret)

Why should graveyards not be disturbed? (The Haunted Shopping Centre)

Can some significance be found for meaningless timeslips? Are some time slips "mis-deliveries"? (The Vision of Misery, Mignonettes & Clarissa, The Nun, the Priest & the Redcoats)

What is the mechanism involved in a Psychic Aroma? (Pungent Tobacco, Mignonettes & Clarissa, The Pilot)

Birmingham

Woman in a Phone Box (Erdington)

A trainee priest, Keith Bolam who was living in Erdington,
decided to telephone his parents at about 9.30pm one
evening. He waited with a young couple outside a telephone
box in Station Road. After a few minutes the couple decided
they would wait no longer, and complaining about the occupant
of the box they went away. Keith waited another five minutes,
then decided to ask the woman inside if he could borrow the
directory. He opened the door and she dissolved. Keith said
she looked very ordinary; about 25-30 years old in a dark
blue suit with a reddish polo neck jumper.

Other people had this experience and asked a medium to
investigate. The medium said that she made contact with a
monk, but the locals insist that it is not a monk, but a
young woman. She is dressed in everyday clothes and seems
quite normal until she disappears.

The red phone box has now been replaced by one of the open
kiosks, since when no one has reported the vanishing lady.

The Ghost of the Alexandra (City Centre)

Built in 1901, the Alex soon had a flamboyant reputation. The
impresario Lester Collingwood provided whatever the public
wanted, principally Victorian melodramas such as *A Woman's
Redemption* and *The Modes of Marriage*. He also established
the pantomime tradition which continues.

When he died in a car accident the Alexandra was bought by an
entirely different character, Leon Saltzberg, the quiet,

genteel son of a Warsaw Jew who had made money in South Africa but knew nothing of the theatre. Under his management the Alexandra was transformed to an elegant theatre offering high quality drama and outstanding pantomime.

By the 1950s, Leon Salzberg had became a legend and stories gathered around him as if he were a medieval saint. His ghost was said to appear the night before the public dress rehearsal of a pantomime in the dress circle or bar. If it did the show would be a success. Sometimes he would tap a member of the company on the shoulder, denoting that they would work at the Alex again.

During the 1960's a ghost of some kind appeared regularly at the Alex. Some people said that it bore a resemblance to Saltzberg's portrait, but the eye witness account below suggests someone in uniform, albeit wearing a top hat. Jennifer Russon was one of the backstage staff for several years and remembers many reports of the ghosts appearance. She particularly remembers chatting to an electrician in the coffee bar who told her:

"I was working at the back of the dress circle last night when I saw this bloke standing there. I said a couple of sentences to him then he b... disappeared."

The ghost usually appeared at night. Melanie Walker was a scenic artist during the 1960s and '70s. She and colleagues often worked through the night preparing sets, and one November evening they had a strange experience.

"One night in the late 1960's or early 1970's a few days before a pantomime, three of us returned to the theatre about 11pm. There was Ken Turner, Alison Gillett and myself, and we heard the Stage Door Keeper lock the theatre and leave. We were painting an enormous backcloth spread over the stage and working in three different places with our backs to the auditorium. Only a few stage lights were on, the curtains were up and behind us was the dark auditorium. Suddenly, I felt an icy sensation as if I had been caught in a draught. I had to stop work, stand up and slowly turn to face the auditorium. I noticed that the other two did the same, though there was no communication with or between us.

The cold feeling went away and we continued work. This happened four times in about twenty minutes. The fifth time I found myself looking to the top of the dress circle. The exit doors had dark red velvet curtains which were drawn across. As I watched, the centre curtain slowly opened. I didn't see anyone come in or out but it closed again. By the sixth time, my eyes were more used to the gloom and were drawn to an exit curtain at the back of the stalls. In front of it I saw a transparent shape in what could have been a military uniform. I knew what I was seeing, although it is difficult to describe. It was the suggestion of a shape, having no form as such, only given an outline and a sense of substance by distinctive brass buttons suggesting the upper half of a man with a top hat where the head would be.

My eyes followed the movement rather than any physical details - as it walked across the back of the stalls and down the side of the auditorium. I didn't feel frightened or threatened, in fact I watched its progress with pleasure, interest and no discomfort. A minute later there came a noise from the orchestra pit as if someone were dropping coins onto concrete or lino. A little pass door leads from the auditorium to the backstage area on the prompt side, and it seemed to disappear through that. The whole event probably lasted no longer than half an hour, and while it was happening it didn't seem at all odd.

When it was all over we spoke to each other for the first time. We had all had the same experiences and at this point really freaked out and had to stop work. Going up to our office in the flies, we found a bottle and had a couple of drinks before we could face going on stage again. We saw no more that night nor felt the presence again.

Aston Hall by night - Jacobean roofs, chimneys, towers and Dutch gables.

The Ghosts of Aston Hall

Aston Hall is an imposing three storey Jacobean house in
mellow red brick, built between 1613 and 1635 by Sir Thomas
Holte. Industrial Birmingham has crept around what is now
an array of tiled roofs, ranks of chimneys, towers and gable
ends in a modest green park pressed between the A38M and
Aston Villa Football Ground. The Holte family sold up in 1818
and until 1848 the house was occupied by James Watt Junior.

The Hall was bought by Birmingham Corporation in 1849,
the first great country house taken into public ownership.
Opened by Queen Victoria, local people visited in droves
and took home stories of portraits with bewitched eyes,
which looked at you wherever you stood in a room. Artists,
writers, poets, mediums, and psychics flocked here.

Discounting phenomena seen during this wave of enthusiasm,
there are three main ghosts. The first is Dick who is rarely
seen nowadays but was well known at the beginning of the
nineteenth century. The White Lady and the Green Lady have
appeared many times in the past few years.

Dick's Haunted Garret

In the roof is a long corridor leading to the servant's rooms
and the central tower, where Dick's ghost terrified the
staff. In 1854 Alfred Davidson wrote a history of the Holte
family, in which he said:

"This gloomy spot, into which just sufficient light gains
admittance to make the darkness more apparent, is rendered
still more dreary by the associations connected with it. It
has long been known by the name of Dick's Garret , being so
denominated from a domestic who there hung himself from a
low rafter in the roof."

No one knows when Dick lived and died, but the room was already known as *"Dick's room"* in the inventories of 1771 and 1794. Neither do we know by whom and when the ghost was seen, but it must have been before 1820 for by this time the novelist Maria Edgeworth was referring to the corridor as Dick's Haunted Gallery. Legend has it that the young man lived in the time of James I and committed suicide when a lady repelled his advances.

The White Lady

The staff of Aston Hall say that this is the ghost seen most often, but so far only by members of the public. The Hall is open from March to November and during this period there are usually at least two sightings. She is described as about 25 years of age, wears a long white dress and seems very solid. The visitor usually thinks she is a member of the staff in costume. She is only seen on the upper floor.

The staff believe the ghost to be the daughter (or possibly grand daughter) of Sir Thomas Holte who, when she tried to elope, locked her in an upper room for sixteen years until she went out of her mind. Her poor demented spirit appears as the ghost of a white lady, documented in the 1893 edition of the Aston Hall Handbook.

The story may not be true, for during the Civil War many ugly rumours were circulated to discredit the opposing side. Some historians believe that the young lady could have been a lunatic member of the family kept out of sight. On the other hand, Sir Thomas was an unpleasant character. He disinherited his eldest son because he disapproved of the son's marriage to a Bishop's daughter, deliberately leaving him in debt. Another story is that he killed his cook with a cleaver when a meal was served late, although Sir Thomas successfully sued a neighbour for slander over this tale.

The Green Lady

Several Aston Hall staff have seen The Green Lady. Late on
a September afternoon in 1986 Mr Philip Bettam began his
locking up round, starting with the oak doors between the
Great Hall and the Saloon. A shell backed chair stands each
side of the doors. He had locked them and was walking
across the Great Hall when:

"I saw this lady in a rather flared green dress with a lace
collar sitting in one of the chairs, and I looked again but
she had gone. The receptionist was facing the chair and
hadn't noticed anyone. A few weeks later I met a retired
supervisor and I told him. To my surprise he gave a complete
description. He had seen her twenty years ago. One night the
alarm had sounded so the police called him out. She was
walking down the stairs. Another night I had been working
late and had locked up when, out of the corner of my eye, I
thought I saw a bustle disappear round a door, but I couldn't
swear to that, it was more of an impression."

The next sighting occurred early one afternoon in the summer
of 1990, when Roy Evans was on duty in a corridor. The hall
opens at 2.00pm, and as it was the early part of the season
no visitors had yet reached this floor. Mr Evans continues:

"I glanced through a window from where you can look across
through another window, and I was surprised to see the head
and shoulders of a lady as she walked past. I was sure I was
the only person on the floor. I rushed to keep an eye on her.
but when I reached the corridor where she had been seen, no
one was there. I searched carefully but no one could have
left the floor that quickly. I caught only a fleeting glimpse
of this woman and I wasn't really paying attention, but she
was definitely wearing a darkish green velvet dress and had
fairish hair. Judging by the height of her head as she went
past she was not very tall, about five feet two.

In April of the following year, 1991, Martin Brookes was on duty in Dick's Garret, sitting by the staircase;

"Some visitors came up the secondary oak staircase and went into the nursery, then came out and went down past me. I watched them go in and saw that them come out, so that I knew the room was empty. At 4.30pm I wasn't expecting anybody and began locking up. Then I had a feeling there was someone in the nursery, so I went in to see a middle aged lady with her back towards me looking out of the window. I thought she was a visitor who had come up spiral stairs at the back of the house, and I went to tell her that we were due to close. She was small, about five feet tall and plump, I should say about twelve or fourteen stone. Her hair was grey with a bun. As I moved towards her, I saw that she was wearing an unusual dress in dark bottle green, tight in the body with a lace collar, and sleeves which puffed out at the shoulders and came down to a narrow fitting at the elbows and wrists. Her skirt looked as if it should have been a crinoline but the frame was missing, so it just hung down. Then I noticed that I could see furniture and paintings through her body. After ten or fifteen seconds she faded away."

Later that year, Mr Bettam was in the Chinese Room talking to one of the staff. They were facing the window when a lady came up the back stairs and asked, *"Could you tell me who that strange looking lady was, who was standing behind you in a green dress when I first came up the stairs?"*

Sightings of The Green Lady are becoming more frequent, two in 1991 and three in 1992. The Hall closes during the winter for refurbishment and one cold morning before the 1992 season Mr Hipkiss was buffing the oak panelling.

"As you walk in through the main door there is a desk on the right and I was working behind it. Suddenly, I felt I was being watched so I glanced to my right. Standing listening to me humming and looking straight at me, was the Green Lady. I only saw her for a second before she disappeared so I can only tell you she was wearing an emerald green dress down to the floor and billowing out at the bottom. Before this I had been very sceptical about her. About six months later I was on duty on a landing, when a young lady of 24 or 25 went into the Housekeeper's Room. She ran out white as a sheet saying, *"I've just gone into the Housekeeper's Room and there was a lady sitting in the armchair. I thought she was a guide and I went to her to ask her something and she disappeared. "*The sitter was wearing a green dress.

In December 1992, a party of schoolchildren visited the house. They were in the Great Hall and the teacher had them in front of her. One of the boys was not paying attention, he kept turning round and looking behind. She asked him what was the matter and he said that he had just seen a lady in a green dress sitting in that chair, and pointed to the shell backed chair by the side of the oak door. The teacher had been facing it but had not seen anything.

The staff have looked through old photographs and records in the archives to find the identity of the ghost. The most likely person seems to be Mrs Walker, housekeeper to Sir Thomas Holte in 1645, and she always seems to appear when major cleaning operations or renovations take place.

Seeing the Maid (Harborne)

Brian Elliott's mother in law had a house in Harborne Road near the Botanical Gardens and White Swan. It was one of two big old houses with stables, cellars and coach houses on a triangle of ground. One Saturday afternoon in the early 1960's, Brian took his old MG there where there was plenty of room to do some repairs.

"I was working on it when she called, *"I've put some tea out for you. "* In the kitchen I washed my hands, then had a feeling there was someone behind me. Turning round I saw a girl of eighteen or twenty with rosy cheeks and dark hair sitting on a low chair. She was in a maid's uniform with a black dress, white collar and apron and white lace in her hair. Her hands were clasped in her lap and she was staring in front of her. My mother in law came into the kitchen, took one look at me and said *"Oh, you've seen the maid, don't worry, she's quite harmless."* She saw the maid quite regularly and had also seen a butler coming downstairs."

"Is that You Doris" (Balsall Heath)

Mrs Davies* and her sister were brought up during World War II in one of the more comfortable houses in Oakfield Road, near Cannon Hill Park. Looking back she thinks the house could have been haunted.

"We had many strange experiences in that house. Mother would never admit to it until one evening she went into a lodger's bedroom and saw him taking off his shirt. She rushed downstairs and blasted me for telling her that he had gone out. He was out, he had left about an hour before. We went back to check his room and it was empty.

Another night, my mother heard a woman crying. Thinking my sister was upset or ill, she started up the stairs and heard a woman running down past her sobbing.

I slept with my sister Doris in an attic. In the summer of 1943 or 1944 I lay in bed listening to the noises downstairs. I heard my sister come home and chat to my mother in the kitchen. Then the narrow shaft of light from the landing widened and although the door never opened, my sister, so I thought, came towards the bed. I was puzzled because she was wearing a white dress, yet had gone out in a pale blue one. She did not speak. *"Is that you, Doris?"* I said, but she walked straight past the bed towards a wall. I turned over to look but she had disappeared. I let out a great scream. Mother and Doris came running upstairs and were adamant that neither had left the kitchen."

(20)

*Are the strange events at Perry Common Fire Station related
to its past as an Infectious Diseases Hospital?*

Photo: Bob Goodall

The Haunted Fire Station
(Perry Common)

Upper Witton Infectious Diseases Hospital opened in 1825
on the isolated heath and farmland of Perry Common.
For nearly a hundred years victims of cholera, smallpox and
scarlet fever were brought here. Before antibiotics and when
medical care was expensive, some patients were not taken for
treatment until the last moment and could not be saved.

The hospital closed in 1922 and in 1928 was converted into
a Fire Station. By 1931 extensions had been added but the
architecture remained plain and grim. Behind high wrought
iron gates ran a long straight drive. The red brick hospital
lay on each side, and across the end was a single storey
block. The holding rooms for bodies had been on the left
and the cutting room on the right. The block became offices,
an engine shed, recreation quarters and bedrooms.

For years staff experienced strange incidents. In the summer
of 1984 one of the cleaners was trying to go through a door
into the Recreation Area while loaded up with mops and
buckets, when:

"I went to put some of my things down to open the door when
it opened wide for me. I turned to thank the person who had
opened it, but nobody was there. This door could not have
opened on its own accord as it is heavy and difficult to
open. I went in and began vacuuming, but all the time I had
a sensation of being watched. It was a hot summer's day
without a breath of wind, yet as I was going past the water
tank to the next building, the windows of the offices shook
and shook, as if there was a violent storm. I thought they
would fall out, it was unbelievable. After that, I wouldn't
go over there unless a man came with me."

These incidents increased during an eight week period in
1991. Few fire officers have been working at the station as

long as two years, but one has been there eight years. He says that during this period the paranormal activities were so frequent and strange that the men kept a record which they called their ghostbusting book. Later something seems to have taken a fancy to it and it vanished.

About two years ago a man came into the office having slept in the residential block all night and he was not looking too happy. After some hesitation he confessed to having a weird experience. He awoke in the early hours to find the lights in his dormitory going on and off. He sat up and looked around, but all the other men were asleep. He got out of bed and locked the door, then climbed back into bed, lying on his back with his legs apart. Suddenly, something seemed to stand on his bed, then they started walking up the bed between his legs (very carefully).

Not long afterwards, a fireman went into a storeroom at the top of a narrow staircase. He collected what he wanted and turned to find a man sitting on top of the stairs. After returning to the store he went back to the stairs and the man had gone. One officer commented that, in his experience, most of the paranormal activity seemed to be centred around the old mortuary, now the residential block.

In 1991 a fireman woke up to see a white lady walking across the bottom of his bed. Another reported that he had seen an apparition which he thought looked very much like Slime of The Ghostbusters.

One evening the men were sitting round the recreation room when the two tone hooter on the fire engine began blasting out. The vehicle had been locked away in the engine house, yet somehow the hooter switch, which has to be manually operated, had been thrown on. Everyone had been in the recreation room.

A fire officer went into a bedroom and saw on the wall rotating images of laughing children's faces. They came out of the wall towards him, then receded. He refused to use that room again. One evening in 1991 eight men were sitting in the recreation room when a rugby ball shot out of the wall at one end, whizzed across the room just missing two of them, and disappeared through the wall on the other side. One officer saw a young woman walk out of a wall and disappear. She looked quite real.

In 1992 a new engine house was built and the residential block (part of which had been the old mortuary) rebuilt, in all about two thirds of the old buildings. Since then no one has seen any apparitions However, the electronically controlled doors of the new engine house sometimes refuse to close, then an hour later they are found shut.

A Pillar of Mist (Erdington)

Bob was sixteen when he moved to Erdington in 1968. He lived with his parents near the centre in a traditional semi detached house built in 1923.

"Everything was fine for twelve months after we moved in, though I did have the feeling of being watched, especially upstairs. It all started one night when I woke in the pitch dark. I could see the landing light come on and immediately go off again and listened for footsteps, but heard nothing. I went to investigate and found nothing, my parents and sister were all asleep. My watch showed that it was five minutes to one. Next morning I asked if anyone had switched on the light but they said that they hadn't.

Nothing happened for a couple of weeks and I had forgotten the incident, then it repeated itself exactly, even to the time. Next day, angry and confused, I interrogated the family and dismantled the lightswitch. Whenever anything strange occurred, the next morning there would be a horrible stench in the room, like something rotting.

The next night I woke in the early hours with what seemed to be a heavy weight on my feet, so heavy I found it difficult to move. This happened regularly, and I took it for granted, but then I had a feeling of a hand moving up the bed. I thrashed out with my legs and it stopped, only to return another night. I was getting more and more fed up, so I got myself a bedside lamp and plugged it into the wall socket. If anything happened I could switch it on. This reassured me a little and I went to sleep feeling triumphant, only to wake in the night to the familiar feeling of a presence in the room. As I reached for my lamp I heard it being turned off at the wall socket. Frantically I switched it on and off, but of course it would not work.

The next day I moved my bed to a corner so that it could only be attacked from two sides instead of three, and I closed my door. The following night saw a change of events, I was woken throughout the night by the sound of movements on the landing that sounded like someone carrying heavy boxes up and down a pair of step ladders into the loft. Next day I asked my father what he was playing at in the night. He didn't know what I was talking about, the family had heard nothing. I decided to leave my door open in future.

The heavy weight returned to my feet, so I decided to sleep with them tucked up. That night I was awoken again, and in the dim light saw a depression at the foot of the bed. I carefully got out and moved closer and saw the dent rise out of the sheets. Quickly, I rushed to the door, slammed it shut and stood with my back to it. Whatever it was moved towards me, I could not see it but I felt a cold patch getting closer. Who, I wondered, was trapping who? The ghost passed through me, an uncanny experience. A host of feelings flooded through me, anger, grief, sadness, and utter hope-lessness drained my body. Whatever it was, it was suffering torment. I felt such pity that I wanted to speak, to console it. To my disappointment, nothing happened for some weeks.

Then one night the hand movements returned and everything started up again. The worst part was the stench the next day and, there was an addition of scratching noises on the wall by my bed. I had had enough so I sat up in bed and said out loud, *"Whoever or whatever you are, show yourself to me then go from here and never return"*.

I thought nothing would come of my speech but I was wrong. The next night I went to bed, switched off my light and lay awake. The landing light was on because my father was still downstairs, my sister asleep in another room, and my mother in her bedroom. I felt quite calm and not a bit sleepy, then I noticed the landing light start to dim, though we had no dimmer switch. It dimmed almost off and a roaring gale struck up outside. I tried to get up but found I could not move.

To my surprise I found that I was not paralysed with fear but felt overwhelming serenity and peace. I could move my eyes but not my head, and out of the corner of my eye I saw what I can only describe as a shimmering pillar of mist about five feet tall. It drifted in through the open doorway to the side of my bed, and though the light remained dimmed, the ghost seemed to glow with a brilliant whiteness. It hovered there for a few seconds while I tried to speak to it but nothing came from my lips, then it slowly disappeared. The wind stopped, the landing light became bright and I found I could move again. I heard my father's footsteps on the stairs and I knew it was over, I felt so serene and calm. I didn't even rush to tell my parents, it seemed so personal a thing between me and the ghost.

I lived in this house for another six years and had no more strange experiences Then I left to get married and settled in a house not far away. The people who purchased the house from my parents knew nothing of the ghost. However twenty years later I heard through a friend of my daughter that the owner complained of a ghost of a white lady who walked a bedroom. My daughter called to ask them about it. A young man of about 18 answered the door and told her there was a ghost but only in one room.

Bob is not the only person to report this type of experience.
This case has many similarities to the Bewdley incident where
a young man was confronted by a elderly male spirit. Both
sound more like the sighting of an out of body traveller
than a ghost. If the person could be identified they might
turn out to be someone who was alive at the time. Both are
perceived by a young male.

Electrical disturbances are common in all sorts of psychic
reports, as in UFO reports, where domestic electrics fail
and cars mysteriously stop. Certain conditions of weather
and temperature create balls and cylinders of air which
become highly electrically charged. They float through walls,
interfere with electrical systems and make "whooshing"
noises. While they sometimes explode very violently, they
often just fade away or pass on through another wall. Two
hundred years ago Erasmus Darwin offered them to explain
crop circles and no one has had a better idea.

Jumping Sam and The Healing Hand (Acocks Green)

In the 1970's, Mrs White* moved with her children into a
council house in Olton Boulevard East, Acocks Green. All
her family heard and saw strange things in the house.

"One night I was in bed awake when I heard noises under the
bed. It was like a woman's high heels, or shoes with tips on
them, walking up and down on a brick or tiled floor. It went
on for some time. On another occasion I heard someone going
downstairs during the night and the bathroom light cord being
pulled. As my son walked in his sleep I jumped out of bed,
thinking it could be him. I went downstairs and found no one
and no light on in our (downstairs) bathroom. I checked on
the children and they were all asleep.

One morning I went downstairs when everyone was asleep. In the living room our small dog, Sam, was sitting by the door that leads to the kitchen. This was odd because I used to lock him in the kitchen before I went to bed. Sam was shaking all over and looked very frightened. I stroked him and thought he wanted to get out, so I opened the window and he jumped through. Going into the kitchen I saw Sam again, this time sitting against the fridge door, shaking and terrified.

I stroked him again saying *"How on earth did you get here?"* The back door was locked and bolted. Opening it once more I let him out, wondering how this could happen. Then Sam jumped up at the window to be let in. This happened in a few minutes and to this day I'm still wondering.

One very cold January night I couldn't get to sleep. I was ill and thinking about the children, what would become of them if anything happened to me, and of my father who had died the year before. It was his birthday that month. The stairs light was on because of my son's sleepwalking and my bedroom door was slightly open.

I was looking towards the door, lying in my right side and wide awake. I felt a tingling round my neck from the back, the bedclothes being taken down to my feet, and an intense coldness as if I was being lowered into a deep freeze. Next I felt as if someone had put a knee behind my back and was getting on the bed. I was telling myself to keep calm and relax, this was not a living person who could do me harm. Next a hand stroked down my face, it felt solid and warm. It stroked my face three times and a male voice said, *"Don't worry, everything will be alright"*. The man got off and the bed returned to normal. I thought that if he went round the other side I would see him, but he did not appear. As soon as he got off, the heat started to travel up from my feet until it reached my neck which was still tingling. I felt as if the blankets were being pulled back up over my body until I became very, very hot. Then I was able to sleep."

Grandad's House (Alum Rock)

In 1977, Dawn's grandparents moved out of their home at the Pelham Road end of Alum Rock Road leaving it empty. At that time she was a Police Constable in the E division, operating from Bromsford Lane Police Station and covering Alum Rock.

"I dreamed that someone had broken into my grandparent's empty house - I chased them upstairs and they ran towards the top front bedroom, then I tried to stop them as they smashed through the bay window. The following morning I was due to go on first watch at 6am. Our first call directed my fellow officer and myself to the bridge by the West End Cinema to investigate a break in. By that time my dream had completely gone from my mind. I was sitting in the passenger seat of the police car as we drove down the Alum Rock Road and I was surprised when I looked up at my grandparent's house and saw that the top bedroom window had been boarded up, and even more surprised when we drove to the front of it and discovered we were investigating a break in there. Piecing the bits together afterwards, it appears that during the night someone had broken in, had been chased through the house and had jumped out through that window. Everything had occurred exactly as I had dreamed."

Dawn's experience is not uncommon. Extensive experiments in America, thirty years ago, established that telepathic images can be deliberately transmitted into the dreams of sleepers. Can we be quite sure that nobody who knew of the break in during the night knew of Dawn's connection with the premises? Did her colleagues who chased the burglar know it was Dawn's grandparents' property? Were her grandparents informed of the incident during the night? If they were, then the simple explanation is telepathy invading Dawn's sleeping subconscious. If not, then she is a clairvoyant Policewoman and should have been made Chief Constable.

Colin & the Ouija Board (Selly Oak)

Colin lived in a terraced house in Selly Oak for many years. His father died in 1968 when Colin was in his early teens, In 1976 or 1977 Colin and his friends began playing with a Ouija board.

"It all started with a ball that disappeared off the snooker table. We searched for two or three weeks but couldn't find it. Later it turned up in the centre of the snooker table. Slowly, strange things started to happen. I would put things down, like the change from my pocket, and they would disappear. Letters would go missing then turn up a day or weeks later in a place which could not have been overlooked.

A year later, my mother remarried and I bought the house. Living on my own, things got steadily worse. If I left milk out overnight, next morning it would be tipped all over the table - this happened two or three times a week. I would get up in the morning and the lights and television would be on, and when I came home from work lights would be on, though I knew I had switched them off before I left. Things would move off the shelves and fall on the floor. I never actually saw anything move but they were often things from the back of the shelf which must have jumped over items in front.

Once it was a tin of polish which I knew had been at the back, and another time two bottles of Windolene smashed on the floor. When I sat in the lounge I could hear the opening and closing of doors, stamping feet and the noise of someone walking across the middle bedroom, then the footsteps would come down the stairs. It was very eerie and uncomfortable. One day, I came home to find that the door frame of the middle bedroom had been wrenched apart. I often had friends staying for company and they heard noises too. I tried taking lodgers but the longest anyone stayed was four months.

The middle bedroom was the centre of activity. Footsteps and thumps most often came from there. Sometimes the door would not open and felt as if it were being held from the other side, then a few minutes later it would open easily. Even in the middle of summer this room was icy cold. I never saw any ghosts or spirits but my next door neighbour sometimes asked if I had had friends in the house during the day. She often saw young people sitting in the bay window. Usually it was a girl but twice she saw young men. Towards the end, a couple of people who stayed in the house said that they felt as if someone was standing behind them.

One night, a girl slept downstairs on the settee and at two o'clock in the morning her screams woke me. She had felt someone lying next to her with their face by her ear, breathing heavily. At first, she thought her boyfriend had somehow slipped into the house, but when she went to put her arm round him no one was there.

I tried to get help and asked a medium to call, but when I opened the front door she refused to come inside. She said the house was so full of evil that I should sell it immediately, so I put the house on the market. Until it was sold I slept outside in the car. When I began packing a friend walked into the house with me to fetch my suitcase. The case lifted itself from the top of the wardrobe and hurled itself at us. That was the only time I ever saw an object move. I left in 1980 and I often wonder if the people who bought the house from me had any problems."

Colin's friend Rob gives his version of events.

"Colin bought a Oiuja board when Waddington's offered it as a game and we used to play at his house. We were joined by Geoff - now I thought the game was a bit of a giggle but Geoff took it very seriously, in fact he was very intense and didn't treat it as a game. After a few games one Christmas, things started to happen. One name kept spelling itself out on the board so somebody said, *"If you are here, prove it by moving these streamers"*. We looked at the Christmas streamers and suddenly they began waving to and fro. Geoff said, *"If you are here, prove it by closing that door"*. Very slowly, the door closed. I thought that was all too weird and brought the game to an end. I refused to play again

A few weeks later Colin said he was having problems with noises in the house, and one evening I realised what he meant. About ten o'clock I heard footsteps overhead. Colin assured me that the house was empty but the footsteps went round and round, then started coming down the stairs. When they reached halfway down, they stopped. I am very sceptical about these things but there was no mistaking the sound.

I was often at Colin's well into the evening and I heard the footsteps each time. They usually started about ten o'clock, sometimes they would last for just a few minutes, at other times they would go on for an hour. They only came halfway down the stairs. Occasionally I stayed the night and never went up to bed until the footsteps had finished. There were other noises too from the middle bedroom - it sounded as is someone were moving about, then there were thumps. One of our friends suggested to Colin that he should hang a crucifix, so Colin bought a little wooden one and fixed it to the wall by a large nail. The next day the crucifix had been wrenched off, removing a large piece of plaster."

This is yet another example of someone selling their house because of the paranormal events, which in this case were probably poltergeistic. Colin was easily young enough to be the centre of poltergeist activity when he suffered the trauma of his father's death, and the Ouija Board experiments would only serve to concentrate whatever he was generating.

The Real Betty Bates (Solihull)

"People keep saying that they have seen me in places that I haven't been", says Betty Bates* from Solihull. "The worst time was when I worked in Greet in the late 1950s. Our tea lady came up one morning and said, *"Betty, how did you manage to get here so quickly?"* I told her I had been at work since 8.00 am. She said, *"I've just been talking to you outside."* Then she described my outdoor clothes - brown tweed coat with a fur collar.

Next day she came again. She said, *"Now, Betty, you can't tell me it wasn't you today. I've just been talking to you in Boscombe Road again."* I started to get frightened. *"How could I get in front of you when there's only one entry to our factory?"* She went away looking concerned. Next day she came again, *"Betty, it was definitely you."* I said that it was getting on my nerves and she started to shake all over, sat down and put her head in her hands. She went to the doctor on the verge of a nervous breakdown and took time off.

I have no idea why she should see me in the road outside the factory. I wasn't thinking about the tea lady or the road or anything. Being on piece work assembling and packing lamps, I had to concentrate. I have projected myself twice before but each time understandably so.

The first time was fifteen years ago. I was wearing a dress with frilled sleeves, round neck and blue flowers. Sitting in a chair, I remembered that my mother was ill, and thinking about her I seemed to fall into a trance, I felt half asleep yet I could still think and was aware of everything around me. When I next saw my mother she said, *"I had a strange experience last week when I was ill. I saw you standing by the the bed with a glow all round you"*. She described my dress perfectly and said I was offering her flowers.

Another time a friend in Kingstanding had Parkinson's disease. I was very worried and before going to bed, I sat thinking about her. Again I drifted off. Her husband phoned the next day to say he had seen me in their house and described my blue dressing gown.

Recently I was using the zebra crossing in Acocks Green when I bumped into a friend, who said, *"Did you have a nice time in Blackpool?"* I said that I hadn't been there. She said, *"It must have been your double then. We had a long talk."* I wish it didn't happen."

Why should the tea lady see Mrs Bates outside when she was working on an assembly line. It could be that monotony and repetition dull the conscious mind and allow the subconscious to surface. This is the basis of a great many rituals and hypnotic routines. Persistent chanting of the same phrase or repeating the same motions has long been used to induce trance states. The monotonous routines of production lines will produce the same effects, and it may be that Mrs Bates's subconscious wanders when her conscious mind is suppressed.

Telepathy is one of the few paranormal phenomena of which there is clear proof, to the extent that the United States and Soviet Union experimented with it to communicate with submarines under the polar ice cap. In some forms, the "sender" produces an image of themselves in the mind of the "receiver". Sometimes that image seems to be real. If Mrs Bates falls into a trance state she does not need to be consciously thinking of anyone or anywhere. If her telepathic ability is as strong as it seems, the subconscious images will go adventuring without her permission.

A less likely explanation is the so called "out of body" phenomena. Some people claim they can travel by projecting themselves as thought forms to chosen places. The evidence seems to be that they are either invisible to anyone they visit or appear in a kind of glowing cocoon (see The Settee).

The Black Country

The Ghosts of Dudley Castle

Dudley Castle stands over the town on a great limestone hill, one of the highest points in the West Midlands. It is now a ruin, partly because some of its owners over the centuries rebelled against the Crown. In the Civil War however, the castle was a Royalist stronghold which was besieged and badly damaged in 1646. During the Industrial Revolution coalmines and limestone quarries were cut deep beneath the castle, with many miners suffering injury and death. The workings were served by a 3,172 yard canal tunnel with basins and branches. The Castle and grounds are now a zoo, but with such a history it is not surprising that it is one of the most haunted places in the Midlands.

Zoo staff work long hours and are often there after dark. Joyce Norman the secretary is sceptical about the ghosts, but she has heard footsteps in the offices when the building is empty and things sometimes catch the corner of her eye. The offices are in a seventeenth century stone house, once estate offices for the Earl of Dudley, and on the site of the old Saint Edmund's churchyard. In 1992, the Assistant Manager was leaving for home when he suddenly felt incredibly cold, the hairs on his neck rose and he was so terrified that in getting out he wrenched the handle off the door.

Zoo Curator, Chris Round, says that for years, Keepers had to do a round from 8pm to 10pm. It was so nerve wracking that they took a Great Dane. In the night the grounds are pitch black and the Keeper had to move by the light of a torch.

"First you had to lean over the tiger enclosure and shine your torch round the pit, which seemed bottomless. It was dug from old limestone caves, and you remembered that in 1961 the skeleton of woman of 40 was found in a nearby cave. The Police discovered very little about her, not who she was,

Photo: Anne Bradford

The Keep of Dudley Castle. Fought over and beseiged, its limestone hill mined into vast caverns, this is one of the most haunted places in the Midlands.

nor why she died here. Nearby a miner was buried alive under a rockfall and the sound of a pickaxe on rock can sometimes be heard. Perhaps it is the same miner who appears in the bear dens next door then disappears through a wall.

Past the leopard cages, the monkey pen and the bird house, up to the sealions, past the duck paddock and into the blackness of the Triple Gateway. The dog never liked the misty courtyard. The hairs on his back stood on end and he whined. The Grey Lady is sometimes seen here. Then to the aquarium, which was once the crypt. There are unexplained footsteps, low muttering voices, and objects moved. Keepers used to dare each other to spend a night in the aquarium. Two did so in the 1960s, saw the Grey Lady and spent the rest of the night with chattering teeth in the barn.

The Keep towered above, and you shone the torch up though it would not pierce the darkness. An old woman once lived here. One story says that she hung herself from the battlements on All Hallows Eve and her black cat was found dead beneath her swinging body. Another says that a gang of youths climbed the walls and discovered the old woman and her cat about to fly off to the Sabbath. Tying a rope round her neck, they threw them both from the battlements. She was buried just outside the walls of St Edmund's Churchyard, where the offices stand.

Your journey then brought you past the shed where my only paranormal experience occurred. I was inside with another Keeper when something large and heavy brushed past. I can only describe it as like a camel in a plastic mac. We dived outside but there was nothing in sight and the area had no hiding places. Another Keeper told me that he had heard the same noise a few months before. Your round then was almost finished, you had only to make a brief inspection of the Ballroom, the Club and the Offices. Once, the under manager of the Ballroom was locking up when he was confronted by a faintly luminous white figure. It stretched out its arms to him and he fled into the ballroom and set off the burglar alarm. The Police found him suffering from severe shock. The Fellows Club Restaurant, like the offices, is built over the old St Edmund's Churchyard. Its phantom waiter plays the piano and changes place settings. This was another area that the dog disliked. He would pull back on his lead and show the whites of his eyes. After a quick inspection, you would both turn and run back to the Head Keeper's cottage to return the trembling dog to its kennel and hand in your keys."

Mr A Durkin arrived in 1987 to work on an archaeological project. He discovered that in addition to studying foundations and soil erosion, he had to investigate ghosts.

The Grey Lady

Two young entertainers were hired in the summer of 1987 and camped each night in the courtyard. Here, high walls cut out noise, in the evening white mist drifts through the doorways and eddies into pale twists. Late one evening they saw on top of the castle mound the dark hazy shape of a woman. This was the last sighting of the Grey Lady by staff, though many visitors report seeing her. Catering staff saw her in the window of the chapel in the 1970's and during the 1960's she appeared to two keepers in the old aquarium.

The Grey Lady could be Mrs Dorothy Beaumont. She was the wife of the Royalist Second in Command when the castle was beieged by Parliamentary forces in May 1646 and died of natural causes, perhaps childbirth. The Parliamentary Commander allowed her funeral cortege to the Church at the top of the town, but not Dorothy's husband.

The Black Monk

From time to time, a monk in a black habit appears. Staff have seen him three times in the past few years, once at the entrance to the keep and twice in the window of the Castle's Chapel. Near the Castle are the ruins of St James Priory, founded in the late 1100s. It was given to Benedictine Monks from Much Wenlock Priory who wore black habits.

The Medieval Lady

There are many rumours of a medieval female spectre. She has only appeared once to staff when she won a fancy dress competition. In 1983, there was a medieval evening with side shows and a prize for the best costume. In the crowd the judges saw an elderly woman wearing a sackcloth shift and grey shawl with feet wrapped in sacking. She looked very different from the others and so authentic that they awarded her the prize, but she disappeared. The officials on the gates were certain that she had not slipped past.

When Mr Durkin arrived he was sceptical about ghosts but has rethought his beliefs: "I have concluded that Ghosts exist in the sense that the Huddersfield Choral Society exists when I put on their record of The Messiah. Where I have a choice of radio programmes I have to tune to the correct station, and so with ghosts. It is not the ghosts which exist, it is the receiver. Where ghosts are identified they are often people whose life was in some sort of crisis, and ghostseers are often people of delicate sensibilities - children, adolescents or those with problems which mirror those of the ghost. It is my belief therefore that by some unknown physical means it is possible for objects to "make recordings" of emotions and play them back to people on the right wavelength. So I guess I shall never meet a ghost, though I shall be concerned at the possibility."

Mrs Popoff (Brierley Hill)

About a mile west of the Merry Hill Shopping Centre on the Hawbush Estate live Mr & Mrs Stevens* with three small boys and an Alsatian. Towards the end of 1990 their busy routine began to be strangely disturbed. Mrs Stevens describes the events of the next eighteen months:

"We moved into this house in 1990 when I was about three months pregnant. After six months, at about the time my third son was born, we changed the shape of the lounge and blocked out a door from the kitchen. Soon after I heard a noise in the night and came downstairs to find the television on. It was certainly off when we went to bed, but I switched it off again and thought no more of it.

At first curious incidents were just occasional, but they became more frequent, until after eighteen months they were almost continuous. Sometimes we would be woken by the sound of running water. We would get up thinking a tap had been left running, but everything would be normal. Sometimes there was a loud crash, as if the grate was being dropped.

The lounge door would open as I approached, then I would hear a cup being put down, or someone washing up, and rush out to find nothing touched. Some mornings we could smell freshly baked bread. The washing machine was sometimes put on spin, the children's toys were moved about, and sometimes after I put them away they were tipped out again.

The house was full of strange noises which became louder and more frequent. In the sitting room we might hear footsteps overhead. We would think the children were out of bed but find them asleep. Later footsteps could be heard several times a day. We could hear something heavy, like a sack of potatoes, being dragged up and down the stairs. There were bumps and bangs all over the house. One evening, there was a bang so violent that our lounge ceiling cracked. I ran upstairs thinking one of the children had fallen out of bed, but they were asleep. It was obvious that we had some strange entity living with us. We called her "Mrs Popoff".

The dog was the first to sense Mrs Popoff. When we moved to the house he settled well and spent each night in the living room. Then he became restless, his ears would prick up and he would watch something uneasily, bark and whine. At first we thought nothing of it, but after a year he refused to stay alone in the room and chewed the handle off the door. He was

terrified of her, and I think she disliked him. A photograph
of him on the mantelpiece was turned to face the wall.

By mid 1991 I had three children and noticed that they and
the dog would watch something which I could not see. Their
heads and their eyes would move in unison as if it was
crossing the room. She would cross the lounge but we had
altered its shape and removed a door, and she walked the old
route through the wall where the door used to be. Sometimes
my older child said, *"Lady."* I could tell by their eyes that
she often stood by the wardrobe in the children's room and
was especially attracted to my youngest, wherever he was, she
could be found. Late one evening my husband listened to my
eldest son talking to Mrs Popoff. When he saw his father
he said *"Mummy gone, where's mummy gone?"*

One night she came and sat on my bed. I thought it was the
cat and was surprised when I saw nothing there. When I was
heavily pregnant and lying on my side she would stroke my
back. Another night I heard movements of someone starting
from the wall and coming towards me. The noise came close
and I felt a heavy weight pass through me.

All the time we asked, who was Mrs Popoff? Why were we
being hassled? Then I began to catch glimpses of her and this
gave some clues. In April 1991, I went to bed but woke up
feeling that someone was beside me, and I saw a woman
over my son's crib. At first I thought she had blond hair but
realised it was grey, and that she was elderly. After a few
seconds she faded away. A few months later I woke in the
night to see a red light over the end of the bed, this opened
out into a blue light and floating over the bed in it was the
lady I had seen bending over the crib. She reached out to
touch me and her fingers were transparent. She had wavy
lines running across her like a poor quality television
picture. The bedroom was cold but I could feel heat coming
from the apparition. She was there for some time before
fading, perhaps half an hour. I last saw her before Christmas
1991. I had bought my youngest child a bike, and so that he
would not see it before Christmas day I put it next to my

bed. One night, sitting up in bed, I saw a hand and arm materialise and touch the bike. The hand was gnarled with arthritis and the middle finger missing.

A few weeks later I was chatting with my next door neighbour when she began telling me about the family who lived in the house before us. There were the parents and three small children, but a grandmother lived nearby. She loved the children and spent each day at our house, despite the fact that she was arthritic and had to drag herself up and down stairs. The grandmother died soon after the family moved.

This would explain the noise like a sack of potatoes being dragged up and down the stairs. I asked if the old lady had lost a finger, and my neighbour asked how I knew. We wondered if she had came back from the grave to see her grandchildren, and finding her own small relatives had moved away latched onto mine. I knew this family by sight and that they lived nearby. The next time I saw the wife I told her all about it, but she didn't want to know.

For the last six months of 1991 Mrs Popoff would not let us alone. She lived with us continuously, crawling up and down the stairs, walking round the house and making a general nuisance of herself. We could stand it no longer. I asked the local church to help and a church visitor arrived. She was having a cup of tea when the footsteps walked overhead. We said, *"There she is, there's the ghost"*. *"Isn't that the children playing?"* she asked. We told her that the children were at their grandparents, and she put down the tea and left. However she did come back with the vicar, and it was arranged that the house would be blessed the following week. We had two visits from the church, a Holy Communion and an Exorcism. For this, three vicars arrived and soaked the house with holy water, it took days to dry everything. Each time, Mrs Popoff returned after three weeks.

I packed, ready to move in with my mother, then the Spiritualist Church said that they could help. A man and woman came, and we could hear them arguing with her, telling her to go back where she had come from; she had loved ones waiting for her on the other side. When they had finished the house went very warm. At last Mrs Popoff has disappeared. We still have strange things happening, footsteps walking and knocks at the bedroom window, but we can ignore them.

The Spiritualists told us not to make any more building alterations or she would return, but we are determined to improve some parts and no ghost is going to drive us from our home. Mrs Popoff had a terrible effect on our family.

My husband and I were nervous wrecks. My older son was two and beginning to talk, but reverted to baby language. My middle son would wake up screaming in the night, and continued even when moved into a bunk bed with his brother. Our poor dog went to skin and bone. Sometimes friends make jokes about ghosts, and I go along with them and pretend to laugh, but to me, ghosts are no joke. The ghost in our house nearly destroyed everything I had worked for."

This is a sad story. A hard working couple in a new house with no particular history have their lives made difficult by an unsought, unwelcome, outside influence. How did it come about? A house with three young children and two overworked adults is a better than average target for psychic phenomena, regardless of any building works. What was it that haunted them? It seems hardly likely to have been the spirit of a loving grandmother. Why, having returned to where the children she loved no longer lived, should she keep returning and frightening occupants with whom she was unconnected?

It is this kind of anomaly that makes it so hard to accept ghosts as the spirits of the dead. Yet the manifestation appeared to be the dead grandmother. Folk wisdom tells us that to grieve excessively for the loved dead disturbs their rest and repeatedly recalls them to this plane as ghosts. Modern psychiatry sees the same situation in a similar light.

The bereaved often hear and see their lost loved ones in the immediate aftermath of death, experiences which, if they go on too long, can seriously damage the living.

The Scouts of Clayhanger Lane (Brownhills)

Ted West has not told anyone about the following incident.

"In September 1991 I was on my motorcycle going down Clayhanger Lane from the Pelsall Road. As I approached the disused railway bridge I saw upon it a lad aged between 14 and 17 in old fashioned Scouts uniform with short trousers. He jumped off the bridge straight in the path of my bike. As he jumped, I saw another scout on the bridge. I grabbed a handful of brake and just managed to miss him, but he hit the ground with absolutely no sound. I stopped a few yards on and went back, but was surprised to find nothing there. I thought, *"I'm overtired, I'll climb to the bridge and look for the other lad"*. So up I went but no one was in sight.

After this, I needed a drink so I called at a nearby pub and told them about it. They said that during the 1914-18 war, a scout fell off the bridge despite the efforts of his mate to save him. I'm usually a sceptical person and I don't have anything to do with the paranormal but I have been tempted to pursue this. I would like to ask round to find out if a scout really did fall off the bridge and who it was."

If anyone has information about a Scout who fell to his death from a bridge in Clayhanger Lane, the publisher would like to know. There are many stories of drivers nearing bridges and seeing someone or something fall. It would be interesting to know whether people actually do flash back in time or whether approaching an enclosed area at speed triggers a reaction.

Is this the least interesting or attractive railway bridge in the Midlands? Cast in the concrete parapet is the date 1969, when the whole upper structure seems to have been replaced. Why should a World War I boy scout have jumped off in 1990?

(45)

Haden Hill House (Old Hill)

Haden Hill Park lies between Halesowen Road and Barrs
Road in Old Hill. It contains Haden Hill House, haunted and
open to the public. The Haden family were associated with
the area for over nine hundred years. In 1878 George Alfred
Haden Haden-Best built the present house on the site of a
former Tudor Hall and landscaped the surrounding sixty
acres into a magnificent park with three pools.

On Haden-Best's death the house was purchased privately,
but in the 1920's it was presented to the town. At one time
it was virtually derelict but in recent years it has been
thoroughly and expertly refurbished, and is now used for
community arts, crafts and social activities.

There have long been stories about a white lady seen on the
stairs, in the former dining room and walking across the
waters of the Southern Pond in the Park. Legend does not tell
us who she was, but her water walking activities suggest that
she used to pass that way before it was created and refuses
to be diverted. She may well be more closely associated with
the Tudor part of the house than the Victorian, though her
indoor appearances are made in that area.

White Ladies, their grey sisters and variously hued nuns and
monks are among Britain's most frequently reported ghosts. It
is easy to understand that a dark or pale indistinct shape
might look like a cowled or gowned human figure, when in fact
it is a cloud of some kind - vapour or mist. That may explain
a lot of sightings, and perhaps the appearances of the Haden
Hill House lady walking across the South Pond tempts one to
believe that she is a misobserved vapour phenomenon, though
it does not explain her indoor appearances.

A Man Reading
(Moseley Old Hall, Wolverhampton)

After defeat at the battle of Worcester in 1651, the future
Charles II was on the run for six weeks, pursued by the
Parliamentary forces in the greatest manhunt in English
history. He had many hair raising adventures. One night
was spent in an oak tree at Boscobel House, and a few
heart stopping hours under the floorboards in Moseley Old
Hall while Cromwell's men searched the house.

The Hall is four miles north of Wolverhampton and owned
by the National Trust. It is 400 years old with tiny windows
and dark corridors. Fiona is a historian who works there and
from her first week she guessed that it was haunted.

When Fiona began showing visitors round many shivered
and said that the house had an eerie feel, particularly one
room in the attic used as an illicit chapel during the
religious persecutions. Sometimes animals behave strangely.

"In June 1992 six of us were standing in the corridor near
the Kings Room. My friend had the family cat on her shoulder
who was showing a desire to go into King Charles' room and
sleep on his bed, which was not allowed. Suddenly the cat
saw something in the corridor, stiffened and her ears went
back. It scared her so much that he leaped from my friend's
grasp and ran off. We all looked but couldn't see anything.
Twenty minutes later the cat came back, unperturbed."

The cat belongs to the resident administrator, David Lee, who
moved in with his wife and two teenage daughters about five
years ago. Like most families, they find that articles will go
missing then turn up a few days later where no one thought of
looking. At Moseley Old Hall these occurrences can be very
strange - such as the case of the missing lipstick. David
Lee's daughter explains;

"Late one evening I sat at my desk and felt a pain in my leg - I had sat on a lipstick in my pocket. So I know without a doubt that I placed the lipstick on the desk. Next morning it had disappeared. I looked round the desk and on the floor but couldn't find it. As I went to walk out of the room I saw the lipstick on my dressing table and it had been carefully placed upright in the centre of a bangle.

One lovely summer's day the following June the sun was pouring into my room as I was sitting at my desk in front of the window. My back was to the room and I felt that someone had walked in. I looked round but no one was there, so I continued my work. The feeling persisted so I turned round again and this time saw a shadow on my bed. The bed was visible through him, he was only a shadow. I could not see any detail but I would guess that he was male, more by the stance than anything else. He appeared to be reading, with hands raised in front of him as if he were holding a newspaper or book. I watched for one or two minutes, then it disappeared quite suddenly as if it had moved.

I didn't scream or run out of the room because there was no need to be afraid, it didn't threaten me. I was more puzzled than anything. I saw the shadow again half a dozen times over the next six weeks. The time of day varied but usually it was late afternoon or early evening. He was always sitting on the bed reading, although at one time he moved his head as if he were looking round. Another time, his head turned sideways so that I could see his face in profile, and from this I was able to judge that he was in his mid twenties or early thirties. The shadow appeared for the last time at the end of July 1991 and I have not seen it since.

It would be nice to think that the ghost was that of King Charles studying his maps, but it bears no resemblance at all to the monarch. No one has any idea as to his identity."

Photo: John Roberts

Moseley Old Hall with unghostly young cyclists.
The warm red brick conceals an Elizabethan timber frame.
Rambling, wood pannelled corridors and small, low rooms make
it a comfortable home for a ghost.

(49)

The Banshee (Wolverhampton)

Georgina Armstrong lives in an ample brick house in a tree lined road built just before World War I. The interior is in period, damask wallpaper half hidden by rows of dark, gilt framed pictures and enormous three piece suites. This is not where you would expect to find a banshee, but Mrs Armstrong tells of an Irish maid she engaged in the winter of 1976.

"When I first saw our new maid, Morag, I thought how Irish she looked, small but sturdy with black hair and dark eyes. She was only sixteen and we did our best to make her feel at home, but she was difficult to talk to. She spoke rarely and so quietly that she was difficult to hear. Then there was a mysterious air about her, and she seemed preoccupied with her own thoughts.

On one of Morag's half days off duty, I heard her leave the house. Daylight was fading so I drew the curtains across the French windows and switched on the television. Then, sinking into an armchair I saw an object hovering near the set.

I can only describe it as a glass pyramid, about three inches in height and its one side was shimmering as if charged with electricity. I was terrified. A sudden hammering on the front door made me start violently. Cautiously, I opened the door to find my daughter. She rushed into the house, threw herself on the settee and burst into tears. She told me that she had said goodnight to her boyfriend, then tried to start her car to drive home but the engine was completely dead. Fortunately she was parked on the top of a hill so her boyfriend was able to push her to start, but as she was moving away, she saw in her headlights a small white dog - then another, then another. She was surrounded by identical small, white dogs making it impossible to drive away.

Before I could tell her my story we heard, just beyond the French windows, a blood curdling scream. I suggested, rather hopefully, that it could be the cat. We crept to the window, dropped to our knees and lifted the bottom of the curtain. Under a full moon a few feet away was a swirling mist which gradually assumed human shape. Slowly, it became more distinct until we were looking at a frail old lady. Her whole form was difficult to make out as she was enveloped from head to toe in a long grey cape, but the moonlight gave her face a pale grey hue and picked out the details. Her features were pinched and drawn, she had a fine, beaked nose, and was wearing a terrible expression of extreme sorrow and sadness. She drifted backwards for a few feet, then dissolved.

While my daughter and I were wondering what was next, Morag came in. She announced that she would have to leave immediately. Her father was very ill in Ireland and the banshee was following her round, and would do until she left for home. We said that the banshee had been harassing us, too, but she turned and left the room. My daughter and I had a drink to steady our nerves while we waited for the next event. Half an hour passed, then I went to Morag's room to see if she was alright. She had almost finished packing. That was the last time I saw her, for soon afterwards she left without saying goodbye.

The banshee is more properly the Bean Si, the Woman of the Hills, or the Woman of the Other World. Her legend is Gaelic and originally only involved her lamenting the forthcoming death of those whose names include the Irish "O" or "Mac", that is, families of noble Gaelic descent. Doctor Daithi O'Hagain in his book *Myth, Legend and Romance: An Encyclopaedia of Irish Folk Tradition* says that she is more often heard than seen, but those who claim to have seen her say that she appears as an elderly woman combing long white hair.

The maid was Irish and dark. Among the Irish themselves, dark eyed, black haired people are known as Black Irish and reputed to be even more psychic than their fellow countrymen and women. Folklore asserts that they are descended from

Spaniards who escaped from the rout of the Armada, but it is more likely that this dark strain is from the Iberians, a people who occupied most of the West European coast and British Isles before the Celts. Their own legends put their place of origin "beyond Constantinople" or in "the land of the summer stars". Some modern authorities suggest Sri Lanka.

Michael Harrison, in *The Roots of Witchcraft* has suggested that British witchcraft derives not from the Old Religion, or the Celtic fertility rites, but from Iberian rituals. He points to Basque as a probable survival of the Iberian language and says that the unintelligible chants of modern British witches have connections with Basque words.

If the narrator's new maid was of noble Gaelic descent, then, according to legend, the Bean Si would seek her out wherever she might be to warn her of an impending death. A friend of the Kennedy family heard the banshee keening in Washington the night before the President was assassinated.

Mary Russon

Coventry

Out of the Circle (Coventry)

Jane Farmer moved into a third floor flat near the centre of
Coventry, in 1990. She found that the spare room had been
painted black with a white circle in the centre of the floor,
and wishes that the previous occupant would return to collect
a spirit or two which he seems to have evoked.

"My neighbours know that we have a ghost in the flat.
Sometimes when I'm out they hear footsteps so they want to
know who they belong to. In the evenings it walks up and
down the hall and makes a noise we can all hear. About once
a month it walks along my roof and on to the next flat. The
dragging noise is worst, neighbours think I have been moving
furniture. Windows open and close, the light to the fish tank
and the video come on overnight. Our central heating has
often blown up. Hair lacquer, cassettes or earrings go
missing. He keeps them for three days, then puts them back
somewhere where you know they couldn't have been before.
Last week I'm certain that I left cigarettes and a lighter
on the stereo; they turned up under my pillow.

All four of us living here have had ghostly experiences.
My step son nearly died with fright the day before yesterday
when all his bedclothes were whipped off. I've had them
pulled off my bed, and felt a tap on my shoulder. Something
often follows me up the stairs, I can feel it, and out of the
corner of my eye I see a shadow. We know its a man because
we can smell his whisky and cigars.

A friend was in my bedroom three weeks ago and saw the
reflection of a young, tallish dark haired man in the mirror.
He throws things at people, just soft things, he wouldn't
hurt anybody. He threw a toilet roll at my friend.

Last Christmas, he threw some decorations off the Christmas tree. To test him I said, *"If you're there, spin the end decoration"* and he did. I pointed to others and the same happened.

Last year I was taping a record. When I listened to it the first side was fine but the second side stopped halfway. Instead of music I heard a scream of brakes, running footsteps and a voice shouting, *"Help me! Help me."* Next day my daughter was hit by a car on the main road, broke a hip and was so badly injured that she still has epileptic fits. I'm sure he tried to warn me but I didn't understand."

The circle and the pentagram are traditionally used to form barriers to hold evil spirits within or without. Jane may have interfered with the circle and released the contents. This case suggests poltergeists, perhaps associated with the step son.

Receiving the Past (Longworth)

Longford is between Coventry and Bedworth. Once an affluent Coventry suburb, it now suffers from high unemployment. Mrs Edwards* moved into a two bedroomed Council flat with her daughter in 1978.

"For several months lights and electrical gadgets were inexplicably switched on and off. My daughter kept saying there was something funny about the flat, but I took no notice. Then she left home and I forgot all about it.

In 1979 my mother came for a few days and said that she didn't sleep well because of a "cold blow". I stopped up all the draughts but still she complained. When my sister came she said that she had been woken by someone running fingers through her hair. I had this experience myself but thought nothing of it. That year my other daughter came to stay and was woken by a man's voice shouting her name.

In 1980 I left my sister's house at almost midnight. Driving home I saw a car parked at the side with its doors open. I slowed down but to my horror saw four youths, and one was stabbing another with a knife. Two of them ran to my car and tried to make me stop, hammering on the roof and windows, but I got away. Rushing to my flat I telephoned the police.

As you can imagine, I was tense when I went to bed and I couldn't bring myself to switch off the light. I must have fallen asleep, but woke to find that I was being crushed by a black mass and slowly suffocating. I tried to push it away, but it was solid. I knew I was not asleep and the sensation lasted about five or ten minutes, although it seemed longer.

Soon after I was talking to my stepfather who was once a miner at Bedworth Colliery. He told me that a cottage once stood where my flat was. Workings had run beneath it from the colliery, and there had been a big collapse with many miners killed. I could not believe my ears. The idea came to me that the black mass which seemed to crush me in the night could have been coal, perhaps I had been re-enacting the trauma of those miners.

After this I was afraid to stay in the flat, advertised for an exchange and moved elsewhere. I have had no problems since. I heard a radio programme in which the speaker said that if you are very tense you are more able to "tune in" to past or distant events. No doubt this applied to me, because I was so fraught after that ugly incident."

In 1874 there was an accident at the Bedworth Coal and Iron Company with three men killed and many injured. The under manager, Mr Addenbroke, was so upset that he left mining and became a minister.

Mrs Edwards suggests that she was able to "tune in" to the disaster because she was tense. Like battles, disasters may "replay" themselves to some people, and she may be right that with her conscious mind taken up by her real and terrifying experience, her subconscious was open to other influences.

What influences and why do some people trigger such replays and others not? Experiments on dowsers suggest that their ability has some connection with the adrenal glands which secrete adrenalin, which makes you more physically able and alert in fearful situations, to fight harder and run faster. Dowsers who have the glands removed lose their ability. If adrenalin floods the system suddenly its effects take a long time to wear off. Was this lady exposed to her second experience because her blood stream was full of adrenalin?

Moving the Hoover (Allesley)

Four miles north-east of Coventry is Brownshill Green. One of its most picturesque houses, with bright window boxes set against the dark red of two hundred year old bricks, is the White Lion. It was a private house until after World War II when it was converted, but it still looks much like a house. Louise Moore is the Manager.

"I'm very sceptical about ghosts but I must say that weird things do happen here. Objects are moved overnight, mostly bottles on the shelves. We tell people that we have a tidy ghost, because the Hoover moves about fifty yards and plugs itself in. We keep the Hoover in the back outhouses and time after time we have come downstairs in the morning and found that it has moved all the way to the lounge ready for action.

A couple of years ago a cleaner who had been working in the old part of the building telephoned from home to give notice. She had felt someone in the toilets with her when she was cleaning. It was such a terrible experience she didn't want to talk about it and had rushed straight home.

Recently I had an unnerving experience for which there seems no explanation. I went out with some friends and came back at 2 am. I hadn't been drinking. I got into bed and switched off the light. In the corner of my bedroom is a huge old wardrobe on legs, and as I was going off to sleep I heard scratching at the bottom of its inside door. I thought a mouse or some small animal must be trapped, so I switched on the light, opened my bedroom door so that whatever was there could run straight out, then carefully opened the wardrobe. There was no animal but one or two clothes had fallen off the coat hangers. I shook them and returned them to the hangers so that the floor of the wardrobe was quite clear and I could see it was empty. I returned to bed, switched off the light and the scratching began again. Once more I switched on the light, opened the bedroom door and gingerly opened the wardrobe. This time I could see without a shadow of doubt that there was nothing alive in the wardrobe. I waited a few moments but there was nothing I could do, so I returned to bed and the scratching noise didn't bother me again. I have never found an explanation and decided that it is one of the many strange things which happen in this public house."

Mary Russon

Staffordshire

The Late William Elton (Stafford)

Fiona Redmond lives in Garden Street, a small street near the centre of Stafford. Her house is a refurbished cottage built about 1882. Across the street is a wooden door set in a high brick wall which leads to allotments. One Saturday afternoon in 1991, there was a knock on Fiona's door.

"I opened it to find a diffident elderly gentleman who said, *"Do you know, a short while ago I saw a tall, middle aged man in an old fashioned suit come out of the garden door, cross the road, walk up your path and go straight through the front door"*. The apparition was so clear that the elderly gentleman thought it was a real person until it walked through the door.

About twelve months later in the early summer he called again. Once more he had seen the ghost walk across the road and through our front door. As a historian, I set about researching the connection between this incident and the history of the house. I showed the gentleman drawings of costumes through the ages so that we could ascertain a date.

The ghost was wearing a bowler hat, jacket, trousers and a stiff collar, round not wing. From this we could say he was probably late Victorian and we knew he was of middle to late middle age. I found that few people had lived in the house and the ghost was probably that of William Elton who lived here in the 1880's. William disappeared a year later. I think our house is becoming famous for this ghost and I have seen the elderly gentleman pointing us out to friends."

The Ghost Resident (Stafford)

No one wants to unnerve people in hospitals or residential homes into lying awake at night, wondering whether the white form they see is the night nurse or the ghost. But in this case the staff are convinced that the home is haunted and persuaded the manager to contribute;

"This home always had a history of a ghost, but when one of the cleaners told us what she saw one day it gave us food for thought. About two years ago when cleaning the stairs she looked up to see a man in black walk across the landing and through a closed door. She could not believe it, the door had not opened and there was no one of that description in the building. It was difficult to see all of him and the sighting was over in seconds. She was sceptical about the paranormal but is now a confirmed believer, although still quite happy to work alone in that part of the building.

Some time later another cleaner caught sight of a dark figure out of the corner of her eye, but when she turned there was no one there. She got just an impression of a tall man dressed in dark clothing.

A lady on night shift was going to the kitchen when in a notorious cold spot in a dimly lit corridor she saw the shadow of a tall thin man. She told me, *"Although I say he was a shadow, he was quite solid. I thought at first it was a patient wrapped in a blanket. I couldn't see any details but his silhouette was clear, and he seemed to be wearing a hat with a brim and a cloak. He walked across the corridor in front of me and straight through the kitchen wall. I opened the kitchen door, but there was something strange in the way it opened, it came much too freely. I jumped back and decided it would be wise to fetch another nurse. By the time we got back the figure had gone."*

Recently there have been several incidents which defy explanation. One of the managers was coming from the kitchen near where one of the apparitions was seen, thinking only of invoices. He saw the door handle of the room opposite move slowly to horizontal. The room was deserted. That same manager awoke one night at about 3am. The door was slowly opening, a heavy door fitted with a fire closure. He had the impression of a head peering round and then it slammed shut. The area was deserted, and the night nurses checked every patient, but they were all asleep.

The room in which he was sleeping was next to one of our cold spots. Several of the staff feel very uncomfortable in these areas and do not choose to go there. During the last few months these activities seem to have increased. One lady is convinced that when she was sleeping, an arm was put around her from behind, draped across her shoulders. She felt so frightened she couldn't move for a long time. After what seemed like hours she decided that she had to do something, and gathering her courage she went to pinch the arm, which vanished. She saw nothing and yet she felt it.

The following night fire alarms went off, fortunately a false alarm. The detector which triggered it is over the spot where the apparition was seen and this is the eighth time it has sounded. A few hours later, two staff were making early morning tea when a tray of biscuits in the larder began to shake. They watched as the tray shook and the contents jumped into the air then fell, some landing back on the tray and some on the floor. The shelf was made of concrete, heavy and solid and not prone to traffic vibrations.

I have been looking through the records to see who the ghost could be. Although I cannot trace any tragedy which has occurred in the home, the description seems to match that of a man who lived here at the turn of the century.

This activity has led to an open forum on the paranormal and the ease with which people accepted it has amazed me. Some staff talk to the ghost and fortunately his presence has not been threatening to anybody. The lady with whom he had a cuddle in the night feels that he has visited her during the night since, and has moved her slippers as a sign that he will not harm her. He seems to have become accepted and no one is too concerned about his presence. After a burglary we are more bothered by visitors from this side of the grave."

The Amorous Ghost (Baswich)

Jane lives at Baswich in Stafford with her husband, two daughters, and an embarrassingly amorous ghost. When they moved here in the 1960's the house was newly built on farmland. Jane wonders if the paranormal events she experiences are caused not by her house, but herself.

She had several strange experiences before coming to Baswich. At fifteen she felt an irresistible urge to roll under the bed, then the ceiling fell down. When she was a student and living away from home, she had an overwhelming urge to telephone her parents. She discovered that her sister had just given birth and was at death's door, and the hospital could not get hold of any compatible blood for a transfusion.

Jane has experienced her present ghost about five times. It began a few years ago; "I woke up very suddenly. We have two clocks in our bedroom and both were ticking very loudly. I felt what I thought was the cat sit on my bed, then get up and sit down again, the bed moved with the weight. Then I remembered that I had shut the cat out. I began to panic and wondered if someone had broken in. I switched on the light but the room was empty, there was no cat, nothing. I looked at the clocks and the time was ten to three. Later, I heard that my husband's aunt had died at this very time.

A year or two later I again felt someone sit on my bed, but in November 1992 they came into the room, lay on top of me and put an arm round me. I thought it was my husband and I pushed him away saying, *"Go away, it's too late."* I realised then that I couldn't hear him moving, so I pulled the light cord to find the room empty. It happened again twice this year giving me quite a fright. In fact I have called in a medium to discuss the situation. However, I find I forget the incident quickly and I'm soon back to normal.

Just a few weeks ago. I was awakened by the sound of two people coming into my bedroom having a loud conversation. I was very annoyed, I thought it was my husband coming in late with a friend. I couldn't make out the conversation but just heard the chatter. Switching on the light I saw that it was three in the morning and the room was deserted.

The Haunted Farm (Shenstone)

Rosalind Prince is Librarian of Blythe Bridge and Cheadle Libraries. She knows the importance of the ghost story, in that it captures the day to day life style, emotions and beliefs of its time. She has written *Some Ghosts of Staffordshire* from which this story is taken. These are personal experiences from her childhood in a lovely old farmhouse on the outskirts of Shenstone, south of Lichfield.

"Its appearance suggested that the building dated from the late seventeenth or early eighteenth century. In the past it had been named "Birchley Farm" and "Owl's Hall", but when I lived there it was "Owlett's Hall Farm".

One night in the 1940's when I was eight years old, my mother came to the bedroom waking me, untucked the bed-clothes and felt my feet, at the same time asking if I had been downstairs. I had not and asked why, but she said it didn't matter. She went into every room in the house, and I could hear her opening wardrobe doors and poking about.

Later she told me that she had been sitting in the kitchen sewing under an oil lamp, when she heard a light step run down the stairs and into the hallway next to the kitchen.

There was a startled gasp and the footsteps skittered back upstairs. She thought it must be me as there was no one else in the house, but was puzzled that I sounded so fleet of foot. Even at eight I was heavy footed. It wasn't me and she never heard it again.

Soon afterwards in the early '50s the farm was used to test the Lucas Freelight system, which was a wind powered electricity supply. For the first time we had electric light at the flick of a switch - provided there had been some wind in the previous few days and the batteries were charged. During still weather it was back to candles.

In one of these windless spells I was going to bed with a candle, carefully shielding the flame with my palm. I reached the top of the stairs and turned onto the dark landing when the flame was suddenly nipped out, It didn't flicker in a sudden draught, there had not been a breath of wind for weeks. It didn't die down and there was no smell. I thought, *"I'll ignore this"*, and walked along the narrow landing to my bedroom in the pitch dark and switched on the very dim electric light. It was certainly better than nothing, and the most welcome thing in the world just then.

My mother had several strange experiences in that farmhouse. For example, there was unexplained knocking by the kitchen fireplace, persistent enough for her to ask who was there. In the hallway where she had previously heard the startled gasp, she once saw a tall old lady in long dark clothes wearing a lace cap and a white apron. Mother was ironing in the kitchen, I saw her look across through the open door into the hall, and a startled expression cross her face. I said, *"What's the matter"*, and looked in the same direction. She replied, *"I've just seen an old woman in a long dress standing in the hall"*. I hadn't seen it.

Her most persistent "Unexplainable" occurred after she went to bed. She would be dropping off to sleep then hear a sound like to a hand rubbing along the wall of the landing, as if someone was feeling the way. Night after night she heard the

(63)

rhythmic rustling groping towards the bedroom door. She would lie waiting for it to come into the room, but as it reached the door it stopped. My father would be fast asleep, and would not have believed it if he had heard."

The Vision of Misery (Stoke on Trent)

Professor Baker was born in Hanley in 1889. Seven years later after a severe beating by a teacher he played truant for a day. Playing alone in the streets he recalled hearing organ music from the little church, though it was locked. Turning through an archway he entered a small street which ended in a blank wall. Behind it he knew there was a big area of waste land.

On this day he found a door in the wall and went through. Many years later he told Joan Forman of his experience and it appeared in The Unexplained (Orbis Publishing 1980/3):

"I found myself in a different world, a small town with houses unlike any I had seen. I went along one street and all the houses were empty. I entered several but came out without attempting any exploration. Eventually I entered one house and going upstairs came to a large room looking onto a landscape I had never seen before. The land sloped away to a valley, I could not see what was at the bottom, but beyond were low tree covered hills. Even at seven I was fascinated by the sun and stars and realised I was facing east,"

The young Baker also remembered that the street in his vision was called Windmill Street. Eleven years later a grown up Baker found himself in western France attached to the 4th Army Headquarters near a deserted village named Villiers Carbonel. One evening he went sketching:

"I came to a village called Misery and as I entered it had that feeling described as hair raising. I was in the street of my earlier vision. All the people were gone, apart from dead Germans in several houses. Then I found a house free of these unpleasant occupants and going upstairs found myself in the large room facing east. The landscape was exactly as I had known seen it before. The valley was that of the Somme, but as Misery is some way back the river was not visible."

Over forty years later Baker, then a Professor of Electrical Engineering, revisited Hanley and the scene of his truancy. Behind the wall beyond the arch, houses had been built on the waste ground. One of the streets was Windmill Street.

What are we to make of such a clear, complex but apparently meaningless episode. William Seabrook, an American, pursued the paranormal all over the world and recalls a conversation with a witch doctress. She told him that the future was fan shaped, meaning that at any moment the myriad possible paths of our future spread before us. If we take a step in any direction an equally large but different fan spreads out. Clairvoyants, she explained, can only see the path most likely at that moment, and what they see is not immutable.

That seems to make sense. Some people fear predictions of the future because they believe them to be inescapable, but what point would there be in knowing the future and being unable to alter it?

Perhaps young Baker saw a place that might, on a different fan, have been important in his life, but which through intervening events became insignificant. In his vision of Misery he remembered the name Windmill Street, and that became significant for the place where he had the experience.

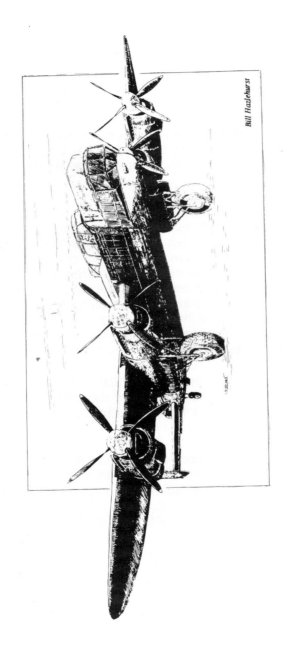

Bill Hazlehurst

Avro Lincoln RF398 at Cosford Aerospace Museum.
A development of the wartime Lancaster bomber
which it eventually replaced, the Lincoln was
the last RAF piston engined bomber.
This one is haunted

Shropshire

The Haunted Lincoln (Cosford)

In the Aerospace Museum at Cosford, near Shifnal there are
are missiles, warplanes, transport aircraft and a museum of
Research and Development. Most mysterious is the RAF
bomber with its ghost, known locally as Billy Lindholme.

The Museum acquired B2 Avro Lincoln RF398 in 1978.
The ghost story started after a visitor took a photograph of
the plane. It showed a ghostly figure in the cockpit wearing
a white polo necked sweater under a battledress. In the same
year a volunteer worker saw something move in the aircraft,
and switching on the lights he saw "a cloudy thing". A short
time later a mechanic was surprised to have a spanner put in
his hand. Noises related to preparing to crash land (opening
some systems and shutting others) have been heard and
recorded, and moving pinpoints of light with an outer glow.
There have been incidents in the vicinity such as sudden
falls in temperature, fleeting glimpses of unauthorised men,
electrical disturbances and turning on of washroom taps.

No one has been able to identify the ghost. The Bomber was
produced too late for war service. This particular Lincoln
RF398 Lindholme was made near Doncaster in the late 1950's
or early 1960's. The only tragedy connected with Lincolns
was that of an airman who crashed one into a bog on Hatfield
Moor near Doncaster. It has been suggested that since RF 398
is the only surviving model, his spirit returns here.

Wolverhampton University made a detailed study of the
haunting between 1987 and 1989. They concentrated on the
clicks and the pinpoints of light and concluded that cooling
processes were the most likely explanation for the clicks and
bioluminescence (from bacteria) for the lights.

The Phantom Ferry (Ironbridge)

The China Museum is all that is left of the Coalport China Works. Two hundred years ago it was thriving and employed people who went home in all directions at the end of the day. Some lived on the other side of the River Severn and to get there they used a ferry.

This was of a type used elsewhere on the Severn. The bow was permanently fixed by a cable across the river. The ferryman swung the tiller so that the strong current carried the boat from bank to bank.

At 9pm on 23 October 1799 a wave swept over the bows and it capsized. Rumour has it that the ferryman was larking about, shouted to his passengers, *"I'll give you a ducking"*, and waggled the tiller. Twenty eight people were drowned, most of them Coalport workers, and bodies were swept as far downstream as Worcester.

One Sunday evening a hundred years later a young girl was walking along the Jackfield bank with her aunt and uncle;

"They stopped and I stopped with them, and lots of other people stopped. On the river was a barge and on it men and women were dancing and singing. One minute they were there and the next they had gone. I thought it must be a reflection thrown from the pub but it wasn't that. So I reckon it was something that had happened there and they were ghosts."

In 1983, when the young girl was 93, she told her story to Ron Miles, a local amateur historian, who captured on tape this rare example of a crowd of people seeing multiple ghosts. Ron says that during the nineteenth century and early twentieth, it was fashionable to promenade along the Wharfage at Ironbridge on a Sunday evening, so that there would have been many people on the path.

The Return of Mr Brough (Ironbridge)

Ron Miles' aunty worked at Coalbrookdale during World War II and she was the first one to tell him next story, although he later heard it from other sources.

In 1926 the Coalport China Works closed with the loss of 300 or 400 jobs. Mr Charles Clark Brough, the director, had told the workers that if they went on strike once, it would be too often. They did strike and Mr Brough, who had been suffering from ill health, closed the factory. He left his home at Coalport House, which was about 600 yards from the factory, and took the secret of his Coalport China to Stoke on Trent. Two years later, finding that he could not produce china of the same high quality in Stoke, he moved back into the area to a house near Bridgnorth.

Some years later the Coalport China Works became a war production factory and Coalport House was turned into a canteen for workers and visitors, managed by a couple from London. Mr Brough died in 1944, the same year that the Germans reduced bombing raids over London. The canteen managers announced that they would be returning to the big city. The management begged them to stay as they were doing an excellent job and the war was dragging on. However they said that they wanted to get out of the house. They were fed up with the ghost of an elderly man who kept appearing upstairs late at night and peering into all the bedrooms.

Many people were intrigued and enquiries showed that the description of the ghost fitted Mr Brough. It also emerged that on days when he returned from the Works late, he had difficulty locating his wife in the rambling old house. He had gone from room to room upstairs, looking round all the bedroom doors.

The Pilot (Ironbridge)

A much reduced industrial area still exists in Ironbridge and
Betty's husband found a job there in July 1965. They moved
into a little semi detached house near the power station.

"My husband was working nights so that I was usually on
my own overnight. In those days, there were no street lights
and my room was pitch black. I was eight months pregnant
and so huge that I had to sleep on my back. Suddenly, in
the middle of one night something woke me up, and I saw
at the bottom of my bed a man in RAF uniform.

He glowed in the darkness and round him there was a misty
haze. He looked like a 1930's film star, very handsome, with
dark hair and a moustache, and he was looking at me and
smiling. The colours were outstanding and the medals across
his chest were quite vibrant. He moved his head and nodded.
I wasn't at all afraid, I was delighted. In the morning I
wondered if it could have been a dream, but I remembered
it so clearly it didn't have a dream like quality at all.

Next day or the day after I was hanging out washing when my
neighbour whose garden backed onto mine asked if I would
like to go across for a cup of tea. While she was busy in
the kitchen I looked at her ornaments. She had a glass case
full of odds and ends and in it was an old, brown photograph.
I just could not believe it at first, I felt the hair lifting up
off my head. I got up off my chair to have a closer look.
When she came back I said, trying to sound quite casual, *"Is
that your husband?"* She laughed and said that it was her
husband's father. Seeing my interest, she said that he had
died from a heart attack when he was 48 years old and used
to live with his family in my house.

A few days later I went into the bathroom and I could smell
cigarette smoke - neither of us smoked. I said to my

husband, *"Have you been having a crafty smoke?"* but he swore that he hadn't. Another day I went into the bathroom and thought it was on fire, the cigarette smoke was so thick. I said to my friend, *"Did your husband's father smoke?"* and she told me that he was a very heavy smoker.

When I went into hospital to have my baby there were complications. The alarm bells were ringing, doctors and nurses running everywhere. I was drifting away and I remember a nurse saying, *"We're losing her"*, but somehow it didn't seem to matter. I was in no pain - I thought how easy it was to go. Then I heard a voice in my ear, *"Hold on, hold on."*, and I knew it was the voice of my ghost. Then he said *"Listen to the voices, keep listening to the voices"*. I wasn't sure what he meant but understood I had to concentrate on the voices of the doctors and nurses. Slowly, I began to pull through. I was very sorry when I eventually moved house and left my ghost behind."

Psychic aromas such as cigarette smoke are quite common, they usually smell like flowers, tobacco or some specific food. If some people are so sensitive that their presence in a particular spot can cause a replay of an entire battle (see The Battle of Edge Hill), why should not psychic aromas be a lesser version of the same thing? The centres acted on in the recipient's brain would be those that define smell, rather than those that produce sound and vision.

Sometimes, as in this case, the smell is coupled with sight of cigarette smoke. Apart from the fact that it is very easy to mislead yourself into believing you can see what you can smell and vice versa, there is no reason why sight should not be linked with smell as well as sound.

At the Cardinal's Hat the heat from a tragic fire is sometimes felt by people today.

Photo: Anne Bradford

Worcestershire

The Ghost in the Cardinal's Hat
(Worcester)

The Cardinal's Hat is the oldest pub in Worcester, a long
narrow half timbered building that seems squeezed into Friar
Street. It is also one of the few traditional pubs left, with
the result that it is crammed to capacity each evening.

The records start at 1518 but a house existed here long
before. Probably the same building was converted into an
alehouse in 1482. It had once been a hook house, medieval
equivalent to a Fire Station. Thatched roofs caught fire
easily so the local citizens stored long hooks to tear them
down if fire started.

The present manager, Rob Talbot Cooper, came in the winter
of 1991. About three weeks later he decided to unpack some
boxes which he had stored in a front second floor bedroom.

"At first, it was quite chilly but after I had been working a
short time, I realised I was sweating a lot. The increase in
temperature hadn't been noticeable but by the time I left the
room it was steaming hot. The corridor outside was quite
cold, and when I returned a minute or two later the room
was cold again. I thought nothing of it at the time,
just that I was having a hot flush.

Some weeks later I heard the story that, at the turn of the
century, a young woman, perhaps the landlord's daughter,
was trapped in the room and burned to death. Her ghost
is said to manifest itself by a sudden rise in temperature.
I have had the same experience four or five times, and
friends who have stayed in the house but did not know the
story have felt it. Previous tenants tell me that they also
felt this strange heat."

Mavis was tenant of the Cardinal's Hat for six weeks before Rob Cooper arrived. She says the change in temperature was only one of all kinds of strange events. Inanimate objects leaped from the walls, and when the building was empty she often heard the murmur of conversation. Several times, she caught a fleeting glimpse of a girl with long fair hair and a white nightdress on the first landing. The girl was always going away from her and she could never see her face.

Rob has never managed to see this apparition and he thinks that the voices come from next door, carried through the joists running though both houses. However, he has suffered from inexplicable movement of items and finds papers or books on the floor away from their original position.

"A large picture hung over my bed. One day I heard a great crash and ran upstairs. The picture hook was intact but the picture had lifted itself off and flung itself across my bedroom with such force that it guillotined a small table in half. If it had landed on my head I would have been dead."

The Cardinal's Hat is not residential, but in April 1992 Rob agreed to let someone bed down for the night.

"This guy had set up a fair for Saint George's day and asked if he could stay overnight. I warned him that the house was full of strange activity and weird noises, so at two in the morning he said he would have a ghost hunt before he went to bed. He rolled up his sleeves and stretched his arms out in front of him. He said he could always tell if a ghost was about because the hairs on his arms would rise. As we climbed the stairs the hairs on his arms went bolt upright. As we descended, they went down again. I could not believe it.

I'm sure this house has a ghost, but a friendly spirit, not malevolent. It's quite spooky upstairs, especially in the dark but I never feel afraid. The house has a comfortable feeling as if someone is protecting and watching over you.

The Phantom Cat (Worcester)

Almost opposite the Cardinal's Hat and tucked away between buildings is the Old Talbot Hotel. No one has been able to work out its precise history because the boundaries of the plots have been confused. Friar Street was built to meet the needs of a Franciscan Friary founded in 1235. The houses were first mentioned in the fifteenth century.

The Old Talbot has a well known ghostly cat which has been seen by the previous manager, his wife and various guests. It usually appears between 10.00 and 10.30am, most often on the stairs in the bar. William Miller worked at the Old Talbot a few years ago as a barman and said that it looked like a large bundle of steel wool which faded after a second or two. His dog was terrified. After some persuasion a housekeeper, Jan, gave an account of her sighting.

"I do not believe in ghosts, I think that people only see them if they want to see them, and I must say that I have not seen anything before or since this incident. However, there was absolutely no mistaking what I saw that day.

It happened in about 1990. I had not worked here very long and did not know about the cat. Going into room 14 which is one of the smaller ones, I turned back to prop the door open. Continuing into the room I saw on an armless chair by the window, a black cat. It was sleek and healthy with shiny fur and big green eyes, obviously well looked after. It had raised its head and was looking towards the door, as a cat would when someone enters a room and wakes it. I called to the girls, *"There's a cat in this room"*, but when I looked back it had gone. The window was not open and it definitely did not pass me. We hunted high and low but there was no cat. When I went downstairs I said, *"I've just seen the ghost of a cat"*, and then several people told me that the hotel is supposed to be haunted by a cat."

Rena the receptionist had a frightening experience in the cellar, which is the oldest part of the house and runs the length of the hotel. She switched on the light at the top of the steps and climbed down. The brewery had lowered crates of bottles into the cellar and Rena had to put them away on the correct shelves (bottling up).

"I was alone in the cellar and there was an unnatural silence. The light cast my shadow across the stone wall behind me, and suddenly there was a fleeting movement, another shadow crossed mine on the wall. It was gone in a second, so quickly that I did not have time to make out whether it was the shape of an animal or a person, but there was definitely something there. I stopped work for a minute and stood still to see if there was any other movement, but nothing else happened."

Miss Morris (Alvechurch)

The nineteenth century Pershore Turnpike road (A441) runs north - south through Alvechurch, but the medieval village lay east - west along the old road between Worcester and Coventry. Bear Hill is part of the original road and is lined by old houses. Near the foot is a tiny cottage, dating back perhaps to the 16th century.

During the 1950's and 1980's, Linda lived here with her sister, mother and grandparents. She had a very happy childhood, but it was marred by strange and sometimes frightening incidents.

"My sister and I slept in the front bedroom and when I was seven, I began sleep walking regularly, about once a week. This continued for a few years until we moved into a larger bedroom which could be divided, then the sleep walking stopped. Grandad and grandma moved to the front bedroom. I can't remember when I first heard footsteps there.

Each evening, the family would sit in the front room and we would soon hear the footsteps upstairs. Grandad would look at the ceiling and say, *"She's walking again"*. I think I got so used to the footsteps that it became normal to hear them. They would start in the rear corner of the front bedroom, walk along the back wall to the other side, then return. The amazing thing was that granny and grandad's bed was against that wall and the footsteps would go straight through it.

As I grew up I sometimes came home when everyone was asleep. Opening the door at the bottom of the stairs I would hear the footsteps, then close the door until they had gone before going up. I wonder how I ever slept in that cottage.

One day when I was nineteen, granny was ill and had to stay in bed. When my sister came home she went to see her, and granny said, *"I've had a visitor today, there's been a lady in that chair with a baby. She didn't say anything but she had a nice smile. I didn't know who she was and did not like to ask"*. Mother said that she had not had a visitor.

Several years later when I was married with two small boys, I returned to live at the cottage for a few weeks while purchase of my next house was being completed. The boys slept in the front bedroom and every night they woke up screaming. They had never woken in the night, so I moved them into a back bedroom where they slept peacefully.

Grandad had died a few years previously, now granny had a fall and went into Birmingham Accident Hospital. She had been there three weeks when I suddenly had an overwhelming urge to get to the hospital. It was ten o'clock in the morning, we did not have a car and had to hire a taxi. Soon after we reached the hospital, my granny died unexpectedly. I'm just glad something made me rush off to see her.

My new house was not far from the cottage and every day I called to see my mother. I still heard the footsteps coming downstairs and now the stair door would open of its own accord. Mother was very deaf so she was not bothered by the footsteps and insisted that the door was blown open by the wind. She was getting old and decided to move into a modern flat, so I spent most days helping her.

One day she asked me to go upstairs and fetch her purse. As I was about to tread on the top step to come down, I felt a strong hand in the middle of my back push me down with great force. I managed to grab the handrail and save myself but I was shaking all over. I did not tell mother because she was moving anyway, but asked some people in the village if they knew anything about the cottage.

One old lady who had lived in the village all her life said it was rumoured that a Miss Morris had once lived there. She had a baby when it was thought a great sin to be an unmarried mother and (probably in a fit of postnatal depression) killed the baby in the front bedroom. Miss Morris was later branded a witch and stoned to death. The old lady also said that since then, many people had been pushed down the stairs.

The day after mother moved to her flat, my eldest son and I went to the house to tidy up. We moved an old fireguard from the living room to the yard. On leaving we locked up carefully, but next day the guard was back in the kitchen.

A day or two later I was in the Chemist's, when one of the assistants told me that the previous evening she had seen an old lady come out of the cottage. She looked troubled, as if she didn't know where she was. The assistant was concerned and looked back, but she had disappeared. She could not have gone round the corner in those few seconds and there are no other old ladies living in the area.

The cottage was bought by a neighbour, Alan, who stripped it to uncover the old timber frame. A friend in the local Historical Society asked if she could take some photographs with her very expensive camera, but none of them came out. On one occasion Alan had found a pile of bricks from the yard in the centre of the kitchen floor. All locks and bolts in the house were still intact, so no one had broken in.

A few weeks later Alan was in the house but the electricity was not connected, so he used a torch. In the living room he heard banging. Thinking someone was knocking on the back door he shone his torch there, then realised that the noise was coming from the kitchen floor. Now Alan often hears banging in the kitchen. Some nights the noises are louder than others, and sometimes they go on longer. They were so loud one evening that the man next door told him to fetch the police, as the house had been broken into. Alan asked if anything significant had happened in the cottage on 29th April. On that day noises became so loud that a carpenter working in the kitchen walked out.

A lady from Hopwood walks past the house every day. One day she heard a baby crying. It was such a weird cry that she stopped and looked up, then realised that it was coming from the empty cottage. She hadn't previously heard any of the stories about the cottage.

I am almost scared to look at the cottage when I walk past, and feel sorry for Miss Morris. I think someone should be asked to lay this poor woman to rest.

The Settee (Bewdley)

John Leland writing early in the sixteenth century said of Bewdley, "The whole town glittereth, being all of new buildings". During the fifteenth and sixteenth centuries Bewdley was a prosperous trading centre for boats using the River Severn. However, after the canals and railways were built its importance declined, which was unfortunate for Bewdley but a stroke of luck for us because it has remained a charming little Georgian town. One of the Georgian houses was Park Lodge in Park Lane. In 1988 it was bought by the grandmother of Robert Millward, then fourteen years old and living in Kidderminster.

"The weather was wet, and I was bored at home so I went to stay with my grandmother in her lovely old house in Bewdley. All kinds of legends were associated with it, and there was supposed to be a tunnel from the house to one of the tombs in the cemetery. I offered to sleep downstairs on her very comfortable settee in the centre of the living room.

The central light was off and the front shutters closed, but a street lamp shone through the side window. Suddenly, a metre or two away and glowing blue in the half light, I saw the figure of an elderly man. He was fairly tall with a round face and losing his hair on top, though he had plenty above his ears. He was dressed in an everyday suit with jacket and a button up shirt tucked into his trousers. A body hugging mist like a blue haze covered him from head to foot, so although I could see him clearly he was slightly out of focus. His body glowed as if there were a light inside.

It was obvious that he didn't want me on the settee. He stood in front of the fireplace, glowering and staring under angry eyebrows. Very slowly, he lifted both arms and clenched his fists as if he were trying to get hold of something but nothing touched me. Then still very slowly, he unfolded his right hand and pointed a finger at me.

I went out of the room as quickly as I could move and made sure that I never slept on that settee again. My grandmother had no idea who the ghost could be. She had only recently bought the house from a young couple. Park Lodge is no longer a house, as it has been converted into six flats.

The description of the apparition seems to match that of reports by people who claim to have seen out of body manifestations of other living people. Probably, if the old man could be identified, he would turn out to be someone living at the time. Perhaps he was a former resident of the house, a relative of a resident or a former owner of the settee who resented its use for casual sleeping.

Bewdley - an excuse for some railway pictures.

The Railway Sleeper
(Severn Valley Railway)

People come from all over the country to the Severn Valley Railway for the sixteen mile ride behind one of the steam engines. Trains run between Kidderminster and Bridgnorth and are largely manned by volunteers.

In May 1976 Alan, who lives in Evesham, had a week between jobs. Being an energetic and altruistic young man, he phoned the Severn Valley Railway and asked if they needed any help with painting or brick laying. They asked him to work at Bewdley station.

"Half a platform at Bewdley is mine, which I laid during that week. I also spent part of each afternoon taking other volunteers' kids for a ride up the line when they got bored.

Some of the other volunteers and myself needed to stay overnight. For this purpose the Severn Valley Railway shunt in old sleeping carriages into a siding at Bewdley. They are 6'6" wide with a narrow bunk and there's just room for one. In my compartment there was nothing above the bunk and nothing below but an old sink, which didn't work. They are in pairs and I was in one half of one of the pairs.

On my last night I went to bed and fell asleep. About 1am I woke up with a feeling that someone was in the room with me. Then I heard the voices of two young teenage girls right behind me. I can't remember the precise words but they were something like this: the first girl said, *"Isn't he peaceful, shall we wake him?"* and the other replied *"No, no, leave him to sleep"*. They had nice voices, sweet and soft, and they sounded similar, as if they were sisters.

However, what I thought was, *"The little sods, how did they get in here?"*, because there is hardly room for one person to stand up, let alone two. You can open the door with a

screwdriver but it is a noisy job and I would have heard it.
I was facing the wall so I swung round - and found that no
one was there. Every pore in my body opened and I poured
with sweat. I grabbed a torch and checked the compartment
next door, then I checked all round. If anyone had run away
I would have heard their footsteps on the gravel, but there
was no sound but the faint hissing from a steam engine. It
was eerie. I did not get to sleep again. After sweating
heavily, I went very cold and sat up wrapped in my sleeping
bag, but I never got warm.

Next day I asked if any teenagers were staying overnight, but
the other volunteers sleeping on site were all older people
with young children. I didn't tell anyone what had happened.

The Children's Secret (Great Witley)

The events in this story gave Mrs Baker* a lasting interest
in the paranormal, and she has provided us with valuable
information for this book.

"I worked as housekeeper for a lovely family in Bromsgrove;
there was a boy aged eight and a girl of about nine. When
they moved to Great Witley in about 1977, I continued
working for them three days a week, six years in all.

At Great Witley they had a picturesque old house on the
edge of the Witley Estate. It had a nice atmosphere, but
very strange things happened. I would switch off the vacuum
cleaner and leave the room, then it would start again. Lights
were switched on and off. Locked doors were found unlocked,
especially to the playroom where the children slept. A door
would be slammed in my face, yet a few minutes later it would
open easily. Disturbances were worst in the summer when the
house felt hot and humid with a strange air of expectancy.

On the first floor was a bottom landing with three steps to a
top landing, where I often had a feeling of being watched.

The family had two dogs, a spaniel who would not go near the top landing, and a Jack Russell who liked to play there with a ball. One day he was playing with it when he stopped and looked up at the top landing. He stood very still, head moving slowly from side to side. I looked up but could see nothing. He stood there for ten or fifteen minutes before he relaxed and came back for me to throw his ball again.

Perhaps the strangest thing was the whistling, only two notes but loud and clear, but no one would be there. You could whistle the two notes and the ghost would reply. Any time of the day or night you could whistle and most of the time the two notes would come back to you, like an echo. Some of us had the impression that the whistler was a young boy.

The son had a room on one side of the top landing and the daughter's was opposite. Each night, the girl was put to bed in her own room and every morning she was found asleep in the playroom on the lower landing, where she had slept previously. She always said that she had had a nightmare. In the end her parents turned the playroom into her bedroom.

One day, the boy said to me, *"Mrs B, where's my batmobile?"*. Joking I said, *"I expect Marley's ghost has got it"*. They both looked up very sharply, quite obviously I had hit on something. The boy said *"The boys at school say that this house is haunted"*, and added, *"I know all about the boy ghost"*. The girl said, *"And I know all about the lady's ghost."* To this day I can only guess what they meant.

Once I was working in the top bedroom and could see the kiddies in the lounge, watching TV. I was dusting, when out of the corner of my eye I saw a figure behind me, almost as tall as me and wearing a lacy shawl. I thought it was the little girl who loved to dress up, and expected to feel my apron strings being fiddled with. Instead something gently squeezed my elbow with long, bony fingers. I turned sharply but nothing was there. In the lounge the children were still watching TV. I went weak at the knees and sat down.

Builders were renovating the house. They were always
complaining that it was haunted. Once I found one of them
up a ladder with his radio on very loud. He called to me,
*"I'm sorry about the radio but I keep hearing footsteps
walking about above my head when the house is empty. If
I keep the radio at full blast I don't hear them. "* They said
tools and equipment kept being moved. They were certain
a spirit level was left on one side of the room; it had been
moved to the other side and placed parallel to the wall. The
builder's son told me that he was alone in the house one day
when he felt a firm tap on his shoulder. He shot round but
nobody was there, so he waved his trowel shouting, *"Come
out whoever you are. "*

My final encounter occurred when I was polishing the brass
knob to the boy's bedroom. I'm certain a lady appeared in the
doorway opposite, I saw her out of the corner of my eye - she
had a female form and was sparkling and shimmering. When
I turned to look at her, she quickly faded away. I was very
sorry when, soon after this last incident, I had to give up
my job because of ill health."

Mrs Baker never found out what the children had seen.
Children see far more ghosts than adults, indeed far more
than adults ever know. Research on child telepathy shows
that most young children are highly telepathic but lose the
ability as they grow towards puberty. Is the loss part of
the natural process of growing up, or is this ability
repressed by becoming adult in a materialistic world? There
would be little point in psychic ability being natural in
children who cannot control, use or understand it, and lost
in adults. Nature is never illogical, and the rational
assumption is that psychic ability is a natural human
sense that we repress. Why, how can this be prevented?

The ghosts in this old house and many other stories behave in
a rather silly, inconsequential way. They move spirit levels,
tap shoulders and squeeze elbows. On the other hand why

should ghosts be rational? If you believe that your house is haunted by the spirit of great Aunt Edna, you may wonder why she frightens the cat, hides your second best corsets or laughs horribly up the sitting room chimney when you've got guests, but if you are playing host to some misunderstood natural force rather than your deceased relative, why should its manifestations be explicable? The wind and the sea are capable of producing effects that are charming, irritating, boring or terrifying. If what we miscall a ghost is really a force of nature at work, why should it be any different?

"Because we love it here."
(Inkberrow)

A large half timbered house which was mentioned in the Domesday book stands on the edge of Inkberrow. Part is very old and the most recent addition was built 150 years ago. The Hubert* family lived there for 8 years until they left the area in 1972. They had two delightful ghosts and even knew their names - Kate Mortimer and Sarah Laugher.

"We had not been living here long when it became obvious that we had a ghost. All kinds of curious things happened. We have a heavy iron knocker on the front door which takes some strength to lift. Several times during the first six months it went bang, bang, bang, but when I opened the door, no one was there. At first I thought it was children and I was determined to catch them. I would rush out by another door but there was never anyone there. Our house looks onto a field I would have seen anyone running away.

In the old part of the house we could hear footsteps. The house was carpeted so footsteps should have been muffled, but these rang out as if on a wooden floor. One week we had two small nephews staying with us, aged three and four. They kept asking, *"Who are the other people living in the house?"* We questioned them and the boys told us that the other people went into their room at night.

One evening I thought we should try to contact the ghost". I
made a Ouija board, drawing numbers and the letters of the
alphabet and placing them in a circle on the dining room
table with a tumbler in the middle. To my surprise the glass
soon started moving. One of the first questions I asked
was, *"Who are you?"* and the reply was, *"Kate Mortimer"*.
I said, *"Is it you that we can hear in the house?"* and the
answer, *"No - Sarah Laugher"*. We asked *"Why do you stay
here?"* and the answer was, *"Because we love it here"*

I stopped the game at that point. It had gone far enough and
everyone was beginning to take it too seriously. I wondered
how much the glass had been pushed. A few weeks later a
younger sister came home and she and her boyfriend went for
a walk to Inkberrow church. There they found a tombstone to
Thomas and Sarah Laugher. Looking through local maps and
records I discovered that the Laugher family was once quite
prominent in the area, and the bridleway passing our house
is named after Sarah. We have not yet found Kate Mortimer,
but some old deeds refer to the Mortimer family.

Standing in the bathroom,I once caught a glimpse of one of
them. I felt someone looking at me and turned to see a grey
shape standing in the doorway. She was in shadow so I
could not see any detail or her face. She seemed to be
wearing a grey dress and hood similar to a nun's habit and
had a sixteenth century look about her.

In the July of that year I had a most traumatic experience. I
took my dog for a walk on the Malvern Hills, and on North
Hill she bolted. She was lost for five months, and anyone
who is fond of a pet dog will know what I went through.
Several people saw her but no one could get within a mile.
Then she seemed to disappear.

I would never try to foretell the future by using the Ouija
board, but I was so desperate I decided to consult Kate Mortimer and Sarah Laugher. I made another Ouija board and
asked them where my dog was. The answer was, Malvern
Guarlford, and that is where I found her. She licked me all

over and settled back into her domestic routine as if she she had only been away for a weekend. Our house in Inkberrow was a lovely, peaceful house with a happy atmosphere and I enjoyed living there.

In the summer of 1969 the baker was making a delivery near Inkberrow when he met an American lady. She said that her ancestors came from that part of the world; her name was Miss Laugher Bailey. Someone wrote to her but had no reply."

The Ouija board was used twice in this story with impressive results. I have spent much time at them, but not to much purpose. The mysterious force that drives the planchette or glass is involuntary muscle movements in the stretched arms of those round the table. It is the same force that moves the dowser's rod. The answers come from the minds of those at the table, either unconsciously or (faking) consciously.

Ouija Boards are easy to tamper with. Years ago I spent a merry afternoon with two fundamental rationalists who would not accept any kind of paranormal phenomena. I challenged them to a Ouija session. They accepted, then accused me of cheating (which I wasn't), insisting that I should be blindfolded. That done, I manipulated the glass for hours to their amazement, because they were now convinced that they were witnessing the paranormal. When I confessed they refused to believe that a blindfold operator can fake messages. Ouija Boards do not put users in touch with the dead. The replies are always such as could be known to one of the sitters, though such knowledge may arise through telepathy or clairvoyance.

Personalities often emerge in Ouija messages, like Sarah Laugher. Often they sustain long sessions of question and answer about their life and times, but they can't handle calculations. An easy test of the reality of any Ouija personality is as follows:

Questioner:	Who are you?
Ouija Board:	B-E-R-T-I-E B-L-O-G-G-S
Questioner:	Are you alive or dead?
Ouija Board:	D-E-A-D
Questioner:	When did you die?
Ouija Board:	1-7-4-3
Questioner:	How old where you when you died?
Ouija Board:	6-5
Questioner:	What did you do for a living?
Ouija Board:	S-I-L-V-E-R S-M-I-T-H
Questioner:	Where did you live
Ouija Board:	T-H-I-S H-O-U-S-E
Questioner:	In what year where you born?

I have never yet come across a Ouija spirit that could answer that last question accurately. Presumably the conscious or subconscious mind of whoever is driving the glass cannot remember the earlier details or calculate fast.

The Ouija Board is not a gate to possession and damnation as some religious fundamentalists warn, nor is it the key to the spirit world. It is a simple psychological and mechanical toy which, used in the right spirit (so to speak), can put us in touch with aspects of our unconscious and occasionally reveal intriguing information. It should not be used by anyone who is nervous or frightened.

Mary Russon

The Dancing Mist (Lickey Hills)

The Lickey Hills are delightful in sunny weather but can be
bleak and unnerving when night falls, or in colder months
when the trees are shrouded in mist. Michael Farrell used to
work at Beacon Croft House at the top of Pike Hill, Blackwell,
and lived at West Heath. He always walked the four miles to
and from work, taking the same route round the foot of the
Lickeys. This incident took place at about 4.30pm about three
days before Christmas 1975. The light was fading and Michael
was alone in the hills.

"It was my last day at work before Christmas and I was loaded
up with cards and Christmas presents. We had been very high
spirited at work. I was very happy and content, even care-
free. I was not in any way in a state of mind which would
induce hallucinations.

As usual I walked down Cherry Hill Road and onto the Lickeys,
took the main path for a short way, then a side path. This skirts
the side of the hill and saves having to climb.

About a hundred yards along the narrow path, I was suddenly
aware of movement about ten yards ahead and to the right. It
was dusk but I could see it quite clearly, and it was vigorous
enough to stop me dead. A white mist about eight feet in
depth, what I could call a classical mist, hovered two or
three feet from the ground above the bracken. I realised that
I was seeing something autonomous of my own perception
and no construction of my imagination.

As I watched, the centre of the mist became more dense and
assumed human form. This more opaque mist which formed
the figure was glowing and the peripheral white haze formed
a kind of aura. I could see only a life sized shape without
detail and the lower half was less distinct than the upper, so
I could not make out whether it was male or female. Then

it began moving in what I can best describe as a leisurely, graceful dance. The head slowly bent forwards then lifted and bent backwards, and what appeared to be the arms were lifted above the head then lowered again, as if in slow motion.

I was so frightened I can't remember more than that. The incident occurred within ten or fifteen seconds and during that time I felt my mood change from euphoria to absolute panic. I took off as fast as I could across the Lickeys, only coming to my senses when I lost my footing and fell down a ditch near the Barnt Green road. I had experienced something that was beyond my comprehension and powerful enough to put me in a state of shock for a few hours afterwards.

Little Charlie (Bromsgrove)

Halfway along Bromsgrove High Street stands the inevitable Woolworths. During the 1950's the store was enlarged and a extension added. It was in the old half, in the far corner of the upstairs stock room, that hauntings took place.

They were at their worst between about 1980 and 1988, but seem to have petered out over the last few years. Electric lights went on and off, strange noises occurred and stock was taken from shelves and thrown on the floor. The ghost was always most active in the autumn and as soon as the temperature dropped he would be up to his tricks.

In the early 1980's about ten people were in and out of the stockroom on the first floor. Some said that when they were alone they had the feeling of being watched. One or two thought they had seen a fleeting movement in the shadows. The staff all acknowledged the existence of a ghost, but treated it as a bit of a joke and named it Charlie.

Brenda, the Supervisor, decided on one occasion to move ladies and children's underwear to the haunted corner. Articles were tossed onto the floor and sometimes moved to the other side of the room. Eventually Brenda stored gardening equipment there but the ghost still scattered small boxes over the floor and occasionally spilt a bag of compost.

The haunted corner had three doors, one of them to a fitting room. It was from here that rattling noises sometimes came when no one was there.

One of the storeroom staff had to make sure that all lights were off before going home. First they would switch off the light in the haunted corner, then he would see to the strip lights and by the time he had finished his rounds, the light in the corner would be on again. Each night he would carefully switch off the light on the emergency staircase, and nine times out of ten it would be on in the morning.

Late one evening a lad named Steve entered the stockroom to put out the lights. The store had been locked up and there were only three people present, Steve, the manager and another young man. The young man waited some minutes for Steve to come downstairs, then went to find him. Steve said, *"I'm waiting for the manager, he's just walked through to the bins, he must be checking them"*. They stood around for a few more minutes then to their amazement, the manager walked in from the other direction. Steve said that without doubt he had seen a dark figure slip across the end of the stockroom and disappear by the door to the bins.

In the mid 1980's a new manager arrived and, of course, the girls were in trouble over the untidy state of the stockroom. Each morning the manager unlocked the door and the floor was littered with clothing. The girls explained about the ghost but the manager did not believe them. Then one night he decided to stay and make sure that the store was left tidy, then to see them off the premises. When he arrived the next morning he was amazed to see clothing all over the floor.

In 1983 the police installed an infra red security alarm and the control box was placed in the haunted corner. Practically every night for a week the alarm sounded, usually at two or three in the morning. Despite thorough searches no one was ever found. It was replaced by another control box which was given strict testing, but that also malfunctioned. Finally the control box was moved elsewhere and worked perfectly.

Every few years, the store would be painted throughout, which took a week. Work was carried on through the night to keep the store running. This happened in the winter of 1988. The nightshift was not for the fainthearted. A young man who volunteered for the job describes what happened one night towards the end of the week.

"I had to work from 5.30pm to 8.30am which was when the ghostly activity occurred. Between 2 and 4am there was a dramatic drop in temperature in the old part of the stockroom. I felt an oppressive presence and heard stock being knocked to the floor. Switching on all the lights, I turned the radio up full, then I noticed it was snowing. I lifted the window to look out on the High Street, and turned to see a young boy standing about twelve feet away. He appeared just in black and white, without colour. He was dressed in a little waistcoat and breeches with socks up to his knee. He had curly hair down to his shoulders which would have been fair. I managed to remain quite calm and watched until it faded away after about three minutes. I was quite disappointed when Charlie vanished."

The young man was intrigued as to the identity of the boy, so he and Brenda searched local records. They discovered that the old part of Woolworths had been an ironmonger's shop during the early 1900's, and the family who were tenants had a sickly child. At the age of twelve he had died where the stockroom is today. Brenda comments that she noticed that Charlie hated stock to be piled in front of the windows. Anything stacked there it was sure to be thrown over the floor. She wonders if the sickly child once sat in his room, watching the activity in the street through his window.

A great deal of this paranormal activity is typical of poltergeist phenomena. Charlie's case is unusual in that he appears to be causing it after his death, but this is not unknown. It would be interesting to know if there was any history of such events while Charlie was alive.

"Poltergeist" is not a helpful name; it is German for "noisy ghost". The phenomenon that it describes is much more complicated and has been recognised since the dawn of history. It has been studied since the Bell Witch case in Tennessee early last century. Classical writers describe it in Europe, and Britain's first recorded episode is detailed by Giraldus Cambrensis in *Journey Through Wales* (1188).

> "Unclean spirits have been in close communication with human beings. They are not visible, but their presence is felt all the same. First in the home of Stephen Wiriet then, at a later date, in the house of William Not, they have been in the habit of manifesting themselves, throwing refuse all over the place, more keen perhaps to be a nuisance than to do any real harm. In William's house they were a cause of annoyance to both house and guests alike, ripping up their clothes of linen, and their woollen ones too, and even cutting holes in them. No matter what precautions were taken, there seemed to be no way of protecting these garments, not even if the doors were kept bolted and barred."

Giraldus, who was both intelligent and a senior Churchman, mused on the cause of the outbreak and noted that the effect was associated with sudden changes of the householder's status from riches to poverty, or vice versa. He wondered why priests with holy water could not cleanse the houses:

> "On the contrary, when priests go in, however devoutly and protected by the crucifix and holy water, they are among the first to suffer the ignominy of having filth

thrown over them. From this it appears that the sacraments and things pertaining to them protect us from actual harm but not from trifling insults, from attack but not from our own imaginings."

In that last phrase Giraldus reaches the core of the matter. Even a senior official of a Church that believed in demons could see that this phenomena originated from people. In the eight centuries since Giraldus there have been countless examinations of poltergeist phenomena all over the globe. All have confirmed Giraldus' points - that they occur in households undergoing change; that they are noisy but never seen, they do pointless mischief, they never actually harm anybody, they are aggressive, insulting, sometimes obscene, and they are anti-authoritarian and cannot be exorcised.

Later commentators have one other vital detail. Always connected with poltergeist activity is a young person, usually female but sometimes a boy or young man, and such a person is under physical or emotional stress.

Every observer since Giraldus comes to the same conclusion - that poltergeists are not spirits or demons, but emanate from distressed adolescents. This idea more than any other has led researchers to query the belief that ghosts are the spirits of the dead, and to seek the causes of other psychic phenomena in "our own imaginings".

The Haunted Shopping Centre (Redditch)

No shopping centre in England has so many ghosts as the Kingfisher Centre. Completed in the early 1970's and all under cover, it is still light, spacious and airy with palm trees and fountains. However, a security man who worked there from 1981 to 1985, says "I have worked at many, different sites but never come across anything, anywhere, in any way similar to the incidents at the Kingfisher Centre."

Most incidents took place within a few years of construction. Local people attribute this to part of the Centre (including the Mothercare unit and toilet block) being built over the burial ground of the Evesham Street Congregational Chapel.

Police records detail many strange incidents. Late one ne evening after the Centre had been closed, a Constable saw an ordinary looking man walking along the top gallery. The PC raced up the stairs and saw the man turn into the doorway of Foster Brothers. Steel roller shutters were down over the doorway and there was nowhere he could have gone.

One night guards heard a baby crying so clearly that they called in the police, but no baby was found. A guard said, "If you went into the balcony it seemed to be coming from Evesham Walk where the fountain used to be, if you were by the fountain it sounded as if it were up in the balcony".

Lifts and roundabouts have started up in the night, there have been half glimpsed shadows, inexplicable changes in temperature, and a curious thing noticed by several guards.

"Throughout the Centre were points where guards inserted a key to show they had been there. One was in Car Park No 3 which is apart from the rest of the Centre on the other side of the ring road. About 3.00am I had to go there through the underpass. Two of the other fellows told me that when it was raining I should keep an eye on the underpass to make sure that no one else was about, then watch my footprints. I discovered that I could see my footprints clearly on the wet floor and the strange thing was that sometimes there was an extra set joining mine, sometimes one way away from the Centre and sometimes the other. I don't believe in ghosts but there was no arguing with that."

At least two members of the Centre staff had terrifying experiences. One was operating a cleaning machine in the alley at the bottom of the escalator by The Limelight pub. As he neared the double doors, he saw a dark shape on the other side of the glass. Thinking it was a security guard, he stopped the machine and beckoned the shadow to come through. It came through the doors, through the machine and through the man himself. He ran to Worcester Square, shouting for help. A security guard says, "He was in a state of complete terror. It frightened me just to look at him. He had given up smoking four years previously but he lit up then."

Another keying in point was in Canon Newton House, at the top of the stairs outside Owen Owens. Fire doors at the top were shut with a chain when the Centre was closed, so guards had to go up in the lift. Late one night a guard keyed in and turned to go back, when to his horror, saw "a guy in a robe shaped thing" behind him. He rushed to the lift and almost fell inside, pressing the button for the ground. The doors closed and the lift went down, but in the mirror he saw the monk who was in the lift with him. Fortunately, as the lift went down the ghost remained stationary and disappeared through the top. The guard refused to go to the upper floor of Canon Newton House again and handed in his notice.

Paranormal incidents have continued but less frequently. The last time the Centre hit the front page of the *Redditch Advertiser* was in May, 1991 when weird things happened in a shop called Pottery Plus. Leaflets and table mats arranged themselves in fan shaped patterns during the night, and once when the manager took a customer to the basement a metal shelf flew across the room.

This last incident did not occur in one of the shops built over the old burial ground. One Sales Assistant is certain that she saw an apparition in W H Smith's which is the other side of the Centre.

"I was employed by the Redditch branch of W H Smith for eleven years until I retired in 1991, for some of those years working on the wool counter. About six years before I retired, a lady came into the shop who wanted some wool which we didn't have on the ground floor, so I had to go upstairs into the stock room.

Reaching for the wool I felt there was something behind me. Turning, I had the impression of an elderly gentleman sitting in an armchair a couple of yards away. I moved round quickly to see him but after two or three seconds he faded. He was of average height with a lot of grey hair and, I think, a grey beard. His clothes were old fashioned, not a working man's clothes but a dress suit and waistcoat, though they were shabby. This happened some years ago and it's difficult to recall the details, but there is no doubt that I saw him.

I knew old Redditch well and I can remember all that area quite clearly before it was developed. Where the stock room is now would have been rented rooms over a cafe which was managed by an elderly gentleman."

It is difficult to find a rational explanation for these events The human race has a tradition of belief in the returning dead and the sanctity of burial places. Prehistoric burial chambers were used for ceremonial purposes long after the last interments. These ideas pervade our folklore all the way down to the Cockney folksong, *They're Shifting Grandpa's Grave to Build a Sewer*. We believe very deeply that it is wrong and dangerous to disturb the dead.

It is not surprising that tales of disturbance centre upon buildings on old graveyards, but more surprising that they seem to be true. Why should these buildings be more disturbed than others? There is a theory that every live human being is surrounded by an energy matrix or force field. The matrix survives for at least some time after death, carrying within it a sort of outline recording of the complete human. Some believe that it remains where the body dies, others that it stays where the body is buried.

It is argued that such a matrix has a wavelength, as it were, and that persons whose own matrix incorporates the same wavelength can detect it. This theory usefully links ghostly manifestations to the dead without embracing the idea that the dead return in some knowing, communicating fashion. It offers an explanation for many events described in this book, but it remains an attractive theory. It is unscientific to reject a theory because it is only that, but no experiment has yet been devised which could prove any part of it.

While there are many ghostly manifestations to which it cannot apply, there are many of which it would make sense. If the theory is true and the energy matrix settles at the burial place, it would provide a very good answer to our question. A graveyard will, necessarily, contain the matrices of many people at many differing wavelengths, thereby greatly increasing the likelihood that a live person in the vicinity will match with one of them and trigger some phenomenon.

Alternatively, there is the question of expectation. If you work at night in a place which you believe is haunted (or at least, built over a graveyard) how far will your subconscious mislead you into seeing and hearing what you expect?

Pungent Tobacco (Upton Snodsbury)

Upton House is described as one of the largest cottages in England. It must also be one of the prettiest. Set in a tiny Worcestershire village, it is a long, low half timbered building with ancient doors and windows set amongst trees and flowers. The windows at the front of the house look over lawns sweeping down to Upton Snodsbury church.

Upton House has twenty two rooms but they are tiny, hence its classification as a cottage. Part of the building was a Norman hall house dating back to the 12th century, and sections were added in the 14th and 15th centuries.

A previous occupant evidently loved the house so much that he refuses to leave and, several times each year makes his presence known by an aroma of tobacco. Angela Jefferson the present owner, thinks that he must have lived there about a hundred and fifty years ago. The smell is quite unlike modern tobaccos, strong and pungent, of a type, she has been told, that was smoked at that time.

"When we moved to the house in 1982 or 1983, the ghost was very active. Shortly after we moved in I was standing on the front porch and I became conscious of this smell of tobacco - so strong that it almost knocked me back, and distinctive. I have often smelt it in the porch. I think he must stand here and contemplate the view.

We have smelt it in places all over the house, but chiefly in the older parts and rooms at the front. Sometimes I smell it in the garden when it mingles with the fresh outdoor aromas. It usually remains for about ten or fifteen minutes then fades away. Recently, mother went into the rear bathroom and the odour was there - mother just had time to rush and fetch us all to smell it before it disappeared.

In about 1985 we had three medical consultants staying here with their wives. In the morning, one of the wives came down and said, *"Somebody was in our bedroom last night, smoking a pipe and it woke me up"*. I had to take her to one side and tell her that it was probably our ghost. They were from India and I think our ghost hadn't seen an Indian couple before and went to inspect them.

He does have a tendency to inspect anything new. When our son was born in July 1987 I came home from hospital and immediately took the new baby upstairs, followed by Slipper (the West Highland White Terrier), Wellington (our black cat) and my husband Hugh. I laid him in the Moses basket next to our bed, then sat on the bed. My husband sat next to me but about eighteen inches away. Suddenly, we felt someone sit down between us. The bedclothes were depressed and the aroma of tobacco filled the room. We felt that he was just sitting there, contemplating the baby. Everyone was quite happy, Slipper and Wellington lay there quite unperturbed. The only person to show any sign of alarm was me - when my husband moved to go downstairs and I said *"You're not leaving me with ... him ... are you?"*

That is the only time I have felt apprehensive about our ghost. Normally, I like having him around. I love this house, it has such a happy atmosphere, and I feel that our ghost stays here because he likes it, too."

Photo: Anne Bradford

One of the largest cottages in England, part timber framed, part brick, set in the rolling green fields and orchards of Worcestershire. The resident ghost smokes his pipe and gazes at the view.

Warwickshire

The Mocking Laugh of Captain Hill
(Alcester)

In the centre of this ancient market town and opposite the church of Saint Nicholas are numbers 4 and 5 Church Street. They once formed the Angel Inn, a coaching inn so well known that Queen Victoria stayed when she was Princess of Kent, It also served the wedding breakfast of the Prince of Wales and Princess Alexandra of Denmark.

The present owner of number 5, Aubrey Gwinnett, has written a booklet on the history of the Angel which includes a ghost. At Covent Garden in the 17th century, one Captain Richard Hill went on a drinking bout and helped in the murder of an actor. He fled to Moons Moat, a moated grange just outside Redditch, and there probably committed another murder. He renamed himself Captain Richards and lodged at the Angel Inn. He was a "well mannered, genial and handsome man" and soon accepted by all the local gentry. However, after creating a disturbance at a party he returned to the Angel and apparently disappeared. The Angel then began to acquire the reputation of being haunted.

The family who converted the Angel to a private house complained of paranormal disturbances. The lady of the house heard her bedroom door rattle and open as something entered the room. The brass handles of a chest of drawers rattled, a wardrobe was pushed back and a chair rocked violently, followed by a low mocking laugh.

An invalid in an adjoining room twice saw a "tremulous mist, oval in shape, gliding along the room until it faded in the recesses". However the best narrative, in purple Victorian prose, is dated 26 March 1884, when "a certain interested gentleman" and his dog decided to test the stories.

He went up to a badly lighted bedroom with his old and faithful dog which, about one o'clock in the morning startled him by a "low prolonged growl". He says that he was then dimly conscious of a "faint luminous centre" which he thought at first came from a nightlight in the room, but realising what it really was he became "tongue tied with fright".

A sound - "like the wintry wind passing through the withered leaves of oak, ending in a mocking laugh" - was something he would never forget. There was an amber phosphorescence in which stood, or floated, the image of a man. It wore a long cloak of dark material and rough large boots, and the face, said the ghost hunter - "Ah, the face comes back to me with terrible distinctness".

The hair was close cropped, the face ghastly pale, the eyes were large and luminous and followed him with "beseeching earnestness". The man later related that the eyes of his dog had "gleamed like fire", and that it crouched against him as he moved toward the apparition, pressing even closer as he actually touched the wall behind it. He writes that he was conscious of his "passing through an impalpable presence", which repelled him and threw him back, before he saw the spectre reform. Then it seemed to be "strangely agitated, passing hither and thither with restless eagerness, and causing a current of air as if fanned by invisible winds".

He managed to ask: *"Are you Captain Richard Hill? Are you at rest, what do you want?"* The features of the apparition were strangely contorted at these questions, its eyes shone, and when it was asked, *"Will you speak?"* its small hand, "delicate as that of a woman", was raised to its mouth before it vanished, and the man and his dog found themselves alone.

During alterations to the building in 1937 a large bricked up oven was opened. Inside was a box of clothing and two letters addressed to Captain Richards.

The Ferrers Inheritance
(Baddesley Clinton)

One of the few perfect medieval manor houses left standing is
Baddesley Clinton. Surrounded by a wide moat which reflects
the mellowed stone walls, the entrance is guarded by a cren-
ellated gatehouse. Most of the house was built by John Brome
and his son, Nicholas in the second half of the fifteenth
century, and during its first few years witnessed tragedy,
grief and murder. Perhaps they left their mark in its walls,
for the building has been visited by many ghosts.

In 1468 John Brome was murdered in London by John Herthill,
the Earl of Warwick's Steward. Nicholas was determined to
avenge his father's death, so in 1471 he waylaid Herthill
in Longbridge Field and, "there, after a short encounter,
slew him". As a penance, Nicholas paid for a priest to pray
for the souls of the two victims for one year at Warwick, and
two years at Baddesley Clinton.

Twelve years later, tragedy struck again. Nicholas, "on
entering his parlour here at Badsley, he found the Parish
Priest chocking his wife under the chin, whereat he was so
enraged that he kil'd him". For this offence he had to
obtain the pardon of both the Pope and the King, and did
penance by improving the church buildings at Baddesley and
Packwood, including a tower at the first and a steeple at the
second. Baddesley tower was known as "the expiation tower".

The priest was murdered in the Solar which became the Library
and is said to be haunted. Here some visitors catch their
breath and refuse to continue. Later occupants of the house
and several books refer to the Library as The Ghost Room,
though the only known sighting of a (ghostly) priest is in
the Chapel. He was seen during the 1940's taking vestments
from a box and placing them on another box in the sacristy.

Nicholas Brome's only daughter married Sir Edward Ferrers, so the house passed to his family and they owned it until 1939. Twelve generations of Ferrers are buried nearby. In the late nineteenth century family events were recorded in the notebooks and gossipy letters of Rebecca Dulcibella Dering. She was married first to Marmion Ferrers, last of the direct line, and after his death in 1885 to Edward Dering.

The young Marmion and his siblings were certain that the Library (then a bedroom) was haunted and called it The Ghost Room. Rebecca describes it as "haunted with noises, whisperings and the like but nothing seen for many years".

Rebecca fell ill one day and her doctor called, bringing with him his schoolgirl daughter. He left the little girl in the Library reading a book. When he returned later than intended, he apologised for being so long and said, *"I hope you haven't been bored"* to which his daughter replied, *"Oh no, after you left, a lady came in and sat down and after a bit she got up and went away"*. No one could identify her.

Rebecca writes that many friends staying at Baddesley Clinton for the first time asked her who passed along the corridor in the middle of the night. They went to or from the Banqueting Hall and tried the handle of the door. The room is not specified, but she adds:

"When sleeping in that room myself I once heard its solemn tread. It had an indescribably awful and mournful sound, as if someone was treading on one's heart and affecting one deeply. I have also, standing outside that door, heard as if someone were trying the door handle twice. It has a very weird effect to hear the door handle jerked loudly, within a few feet of where you are standing, and see no one."

One July night in 1887, Rebecca's cousin, Constance Croxton, was sleeping in the State Bedroom (now Henry Ferrer's room);

"I suddenly woke up with the feeling of something not human being in the room, and saw distinctly in the moonlight, a figure in black with bright golden hair standing near the writing table, his face was towards me, it seemed to me to have the Ferrers features and was peaceful looking, as if also in deep thought. The figure disappeared soon after I had seen it. I think this must be the same figure I saw one night in the Tapestry room. I awoke again with that feeling of something supernatural being in the room and I saw clearly a dark figure glide by my bed and out of the door."

The following month another friend of Rebecca's, Kate Fetherston, spent the night in the Banqueting Hall. Her narrative is pasted into one of Rebecca's notebooks.

"I had been asleep and was broad awake when, turning to the corner of the room where the nightlight stands on my washhand table and lights up the picture of our Blessed Lady that hangs above, I saw, to my surprise, the picture of an officer instead of her, it was as if he came in front of the picture and obscured all but a bit of landscape at the side. He was in scarlet uniform with a white belt across the breast, the features were dim and shadowy. It remained a long time. When I woke again it was still there. At last it disappeared and I saw the picture of our Blessed Lady distinct as usual."

When she told Rebecca about her experience, Rebecca remembered that she had a miniature of Major Thomas Ferrers, who had died seventy years previously. He was wearing a scarlet uniform with a white horizontal band. When she examined the tiny portrait she found with it a scrap of paper which said that the Major had served through the Peninsular War without injury but was killed in 1817 when he fell from the ramparts at Cambray. The Ferrers were a very handsome family, with golden hair, soft grey eyes, black arched eyebrows and beautifully chiselled lips. Kate had no difficulty in identifying her ghost as the Major. No other Ferrers had worn this distinctive uniform.

Rebecca and her friends seem to be quite relaxed about the appearance of these ghosts, even going off to sleep with an apparition in the room. Rebecca regards them with great compassion, believing that each spirit represents a poor soul who is in urgent need of prayers and masses. She arranged with the Presbytery Priest that this should be done and later remarks that the strange footsteps ceased.

About seventeen years later her notebooks contain a dramatic entry, headed SEQUEL. It is late autumn and Rebecca has invited to Baddesley a party of four, Mr James Cumberland, Francis Radford and two women. Mr Cumberland is sleeping in the Blue Room and Francis next door in the Tapestry Room.

"Mr Cumberland only came for 2 days and the morning after his arrival, came down looking pale and uncomfortable; and later on, owned that he had had a very miserable night. He was awoke by hearing a sound as if someone were walking along the passage outside and feeling or scraping against the wall, then the steps appeared to go into the next room, where Francis Rudford was, and then there came a loud violent noise, as if somebody had taken off heavy boots in that room and flung them down on the floor. Mr Cumberland thought that Francis must be ill, and kept himself awake for a little expecting to be called up to help. The Stable Clock struck twelve, but all remained quiet so he fell asleep.

Some time afterwards he woke up suddenly with a feeling of something in the room. The Clock was striking four. The moonlight was streaming in through the Eastern windows and made the room quite light. However opposite to his bed was a picture distinctly seen as if with a light of its own. He wondered for a few minutes, thinking that he had not before noticed it and then remembered that when he went to bed a wardrobe had been there. The picture was that of a young officer with a white belt across his breast. A wide gilt frame was enclosing it. As he looked the whole thing seemed to come towards him close to the bottom of the bed he looked again and nothing was to be seen."

Rebecca adds that Francis has spent the night undisturbed and stresses that Mr Cumberland was a recent acquaintance who, like Kate Fetherston, knew nothing of the ghost or Major Ferrers. She arranges for more masses and prayers.

Major Thomas Ferrers was not laid to rest. At the beginning of this century Miss Henrietta Knight was woken by the sound of several people arriving at her door. The footsteps were followed by a rapping sound emanating from the floors and ceiling. She then heard a noise in her room, as of cloth being torn, followed by breathing close to her ear.

One more ghost has been seen. "A very pretty lady, young and in black" has occasionally appeared. Perhaps this is the spirit seen by the doctor's daughter in the library.

In 1884 a guest sleeping in the Tapestry Room found herself awake in time to see a fair haired woman in black glide past her bed and vanish through a locked door. Three years later she stayed again and this time slept in the State Bedroom. Again she saw the same woman glide past her bed.

A mysterious paragraph in a letter to Rebecca dated August 1894 from Father Fairfax of Oulton Abbey, an old family friend, reads, "I hope to say mass on Friday for the poor one I saw seated in the hall on Thursday last". Rebecca has written an explanation across the last page;

"After luncheon last Thursday, when we had all dispersed, Father Fairfax passed through the hall to go to his room. It was about 4 o'clock, when to his surprise he saw a young lady, pensive and sad, sitting on the sofa in the hall. He passed close to her expecting her to look up or speak, but she took no notice. There was no one in the house, he said, who at all resembled her: four little girls who had come to luncheon another day saw her there: also Kate Fetherston (in the afternoon)."

It may be that this young woman is the wife of Nicholas Brome or one of the women who risked their lives by hiding priests during the anti Catholic mania of the late sixteenth century. In October 1591 the house was searched for four hours by priest hunters, but the priests were well hidden in the specially adapted kitchen drain.

Finally, Cecil Ralph Ferrers lived at the house for a period before it became National Trust property. A friend who often came for supper noticed that his little dog used to sit up and beg to an empty chair. When he asked Cecil the reason for this, he said, *"That's the ghost's chair, I never sit in that chair myself"*.

The Strange People at Guy's Cliff (Warwick)

Warwick, not Stratford, was the place of pilgrimage in the middle ages, when people came in hundreds to the cave at Guy's Cliffe where Guy of Warwick spent his last days. A ballad told how Guy fought the Danish champion to save England from the invaders, then aged and battle scarred, he would not reveal himself to his beautiful wife Felice, daughter of the Earl of Warwick. He lived in the cave as a hermit but near the end sent his ring to Felice, who hastened to see him. Naturally, she was too late, and overcome with grief threw herself over the cliff into the River Avon.

About half a mile from Guy's Cliff is Blacklow Hill where Piers Gavaston, favourite of Edward II, was killed in 1312 by a later Earl of Warwick (The Black Dog of Arden).

Guy's Cliff Manor is the crumbling ruin of a spectacular Palladian house which clings to the cliff. Nearby is a riding school which the owner, Janet, explains was developed from the old Manor coach horse stables. She adds:

"This whole area is extremely beautiful and steeped in history. I am sure it is haunted by the past. One local legend tells of a White Lady near Guy's Cliff, thought to be Felice. Anther tale is of a funeral cortege winding its way down Blacklow Hill on foggy evenings. We hear all kinds of unusual noises and sometimes I feel as if someone is watching me, but when I turn round no one is there.

I hear all kinds of strange stories from other people. A few years ago some girls were staying here during the summer months in the old stable which has been converted into a dormitory. They said that they had seen a man in strange clothes going through the door at the end. I said they must have seen the gardener, but they insisted that this was someone quite different. He had a strange light glowing all round him and wore a top hat, a tailcoat and a frilly cravat.

This incident reminded me that I had seen a similar apparition by my bed in 1963. I woke up in the night to find a man dressed as the girls described standing by my bed. In one hand he held a pair of gloves which were laid across the other hand. I yelled and he disappeared. He looked very much like sketches of Piers Gaveston which I have seen.

This was not my first nocturnal visitor. Before we came here I had never seen a ghost or given them a thought, but I have now seen several. Three months after we moved in I was lying in bed with my five year old daughter when I felt someone come into the room. I thought it was my ex husband and waited for him to say something. Nothing was said and I still felt he was there, so I turned and saw, at the end of the bed, a lady dressed in white. She had a cord round her waist and her neck was crossed with fine tape. Her head was covered with a headscarf tied in a very elegant fashion, and I could just see blond hair. The apparition was looking at my daughter, and when I screamed it slowly rose into the air and floated towards her. My one thought was that I must protect my child but I could not move, I felt paralysed. I screamed again and this time my ex husband came running upstairs. He told me later that I was sitting up in bed talking gibberish, saying *"I saw it, I did see it."* The room had become freezing cold and I was like ice, yet my hands were sweating.

Guy's Cliff Manor, magnificent and mysterious ruin perched on a cliff. Below is the cave where Guy of Warwick lived as a hermit and died, and his wife killed herself. But who or what now haunts the stables?

(111)

My daughter was due to go into hospital the next day and I thought this could be a premonition that I should not take her. However my husband said that perhaps this was a good ghost who had come to bless her. My daughter did develop bronchitis after the operation but recovered.

About a year later, when my daughter was six, I went into her room to say goodnight and found her lying with the bed covers over her head. She explained, *"It's because of the white lady, I don't like her"*. She told me that this white lady came into her room every night and looked at her. I asked her how long this had been going on and she replied, *"For years"*.

A few years later, some young teenagers who were staying in the dormitory banged on my door at midnight to tell me that they had seen the ghost of a white lady walking across the courtyard. She was seen by a group of foreign girls in the summer of 1984, and I have since seen her twice in the house.

One evening in the late 1980's, I saw two ghosts. I was sitting up in bed with my small son sleeping at my side. He was restless and kept mumbling, tossing and turning and getting up on all fours. Then I saw a tiny spot of light on the other side of the room coming slowly towards me. I thought, *"Don't be alarmed, study it"*. It took ages to reach me, then it suddenly went whoosh to one side and there stood a man in Victorian dress. He was quite chubby with tight curly brown hair, one earring, an open leather waistcoat and a leather belt, and he was laughing at me. I braced myself against the wall and stared at him until he disappeared.

The second apparition came soon afterwards but was not at all frightening. It was a young child of five or six, his head just above the height of the bed, but he could have been kneeling. He too had tight curly hair and he was laughing at my son, but I couldn't hear him. He was wearing a Victorian blouse. After the second apparition had disappeared, my son settled into a deep, peaceful sleep.

Despite these strange occurrences I am not afraid to walk around alone at night. The area is so beautiful; from our house a rhododendron walk reaches down to the edge of the cliff and there is a croquet lawn. Both are overgrown but you can imagine ladies in floor length skirts walking along them. There is an atmosphere of peace and tranquillity and I know that if there is a presence here, it is friendly."

Simon Returns (Leamington Spa)

Not many years ago Mrs Hastings* and her husband retired. They are well known in the Leamington area, Mrs Hastings has been involved in local social work, and Mr Hastings has been curator of several public buildings. She has an intriguing anecdote to tell about her only child, now in his thirties.

"My son Simon was born at Frankton, which is about a mile south of Stretton on Dunsmore. Even as a baby he was quiet and thoughtful, not boisterous like the other small boys. He seemed delicate and was often poorly. One of his first ill-nesses as a baby was a nasty attack of pharyngitis. It was pitiful to watch him trying to breathe, I was so worried that I sat by his cot most of the day and the night. I would rush off and do some housework then rush back. One evening I changed Simon into his best romper suit with blue windmills, then rushed away to cook. I was away longer than usual.

Returning to the bedroom I felt this lovely glow, as if the fire were burning well. A young man was standing in the semi darkness beside the cot. He was aged about seventeen, a good six feet tall with dark hair and wearing a tweed jacket. He was just looking at the baby. With alarm I looked at Simon too, but he just put his little fat hand to his face and turned over. The figure vanished quite suddenly. I hurried to the cot but there was no need to worry, the stertorous breathing had stopped and Simon was lying there with a healthy colour in his cheeks. The change was so remarkable that I fetched my husband to have a look. I said, *"It must have been his guardian angel."*

(113)

As the years went by my son left behind his ill health and to everyone's surprise, became a 100 metre sprint champion, often running for Warwickshire. Then, when he was seventeen, his leg was smashed in a traffic accident which ended his sprinting career. I brought him home from Warwick Hospital, by this time we had moved to a maisonette in Barford. His leg was in plaster and I could see that he was very depressed. He leaned on the mantelpiece and looked into the fire, then he seemed to become mesmerised by something in the fireplace. As I watched I realised that here was a tall, dark haired, seventeen year old in a tweed jacket - here was my ghost. I asked him, *"What can you see in the fire, Simon?"* and he replied, *"There's a sick baby, oh what a shame, I wish it were better."* I asked him what the baby was wearing and he answered, *"It's got blue windmills all over its nighty"*.

Mrs Hastings gives us a moving and satisfying story. So many true stories of the paranormal are unsatisfactory, trivial or pointless or lacking any kind of rationale. This tale has a point and balance that is almost unique. Here is the mother, twice concerned for her son and twice comforted. Here is the boy, twice unhappy and twice in touch with another self.

Because it is so neat and complete, one looks for meaning. The idea that ghosts seen in childhood may be manifestations of one's later self has attracted writers of fiction but is, largely absent from traditional tales or contemporary accounts.

Several adults who were unhappy in childhood have told me that when times are hard, they see themselves as children and sometimes speak to their other self. They are supported by the recollection that they have survived worse days when they were less able. The comedian Billy Connolly said in a recent television interview that he holds conversations with his childhood self.

It has been argued for a long time that apparent ability to see into the past or future arises because time is not a straight line, on which events are separated by known distances. Time may be spiral, so certain points are much closer together than we expect, and passage between them occurs like a record pickup jumping a groove. Another theory suggests that all points in time are in touch with each other; that the mechanisms guiding our path through certain points sometimes fault and place us in the past or future. These theories would barely explain this case. If Simon's appearances to himself were random accidents of the machinery of time, they would be the most astonishing coincidences of all time.

If there is a real connection between the two events, what can it be? Do they not imply that the nature of human existence is even more complex than we thought? Do they indicate that human personality, the soul, the psyche, or whatever you label it, has some overiding structure outside what we understand as time, and able to communicate with itself along or across the ordinary time stream? We are not trying to put any religion into or out of business with any concept of an after life. We are suggesting that, within its earthly existence the human being has the ability to move forward and backward within its own time when it needs to.

Mary Russon

Mignonnettes & Clarissa
(Leamington Spa)

In 1977 Mr and Mrs Herbert* bought an eight bedroomed house off Tachbrook Road in Leamington from an Indian family. When the sale was completed, the man said, *"We're glad you bought the house, we felt you were the right people for it. If you hadn't bought it, we wouldn't have sold."* Mr Herbert says:

"We have often wondered if this remark had anything to do with events that followed. We later asked the Indian family about them but the husband replied, *"We never saw anything like that but my son would never come up to the front of the house as he said it was always cold".*

When we looked over the house I could smell mignonettes, a delightful perfume. I thought it must be Indian and thought nothing of it, but the odour remained long after the family had left. I planted some in the garden and my wife placed a posy on the kitchen window ledge. Four months later the flowers were still fresh and the leaves still soft and green.

Not long after we moved in I caught flu. Lying in bed with my eyes closed I felt someone put a blanket over me and tuck me in. I murmured *"Thank you"* and drifted off to sleep. Later, I mentioned this to my wife and she said that she had been the only person in the house, and she hadn't covered me.

We had a cat called Boris and one day, I walked into the hallway to see him halfway up the stairs on his hind legs and playing with an invisible something in mid air. It was so strange that I fetched my wife to look.

This house had three floors, and each landing was fitted with a press button light switch which turned itself off after a many minutes. One evening, the switches kept turning themselves on and off. I walked across the top landing and just as I got my hand to the switch it turned itself off.

We had two lads staying with us, Eric and Jim, and the next morning Eric said, *"I heard you going upstairs last night. Who was the lady who went with you in the high heels.?"* Hastily I said that no female had accompanied me upstairs that night, but Jim said he heard it, too. I pointed out that this was impossible as we had carpet and noises would be muffled, which mystified them. They said that the footsteps rang out as if they were on lino. I told them about the light switches and they remarked that my story wasn't true, no one could reach the upstairs lightswitch because there was a huge table in front of it. Then it was my turn to be mystified. I had certainly put my hand on the switch the previous evening, I must have walked through the table."

The story is continued by Mrs Herbert;

"I learned from Archie our local greengrocer, who was 85, that the Station Master had built the house and later sold it to the Postmaster of Leamington, or vice versa. He said that when he was a lad a lovely lass named Clarissa lived in the house and he secretly went out with her a few times. When her father found out he was barred because he was Trade, and he was hammered by his dad because they lost a good order.

We altered the kitchen which made a lot of work and when we had finished I almost slept the clock round. In the late afternoon I made myself get up, and although still sleepy I decided to write to my mother. I finished the first page, turned over and numbered it, then turned back to see what my last sentence had been. In beautiful copperplate and written over my handwriting was a name, Clarissa Steadman. I thought perhaps I might have written it in my sleepy state, but the two inks were different.

Eric and Jim left us and were replaced by a young man who worked for a furniture company. One day, he said, *"There's a funny bloke in my bedroom, he walked up to me, took off his top hat and asked me where the hall stand was."* With that, he burst into tears and asked if he could be moved to another bedroom. He wasn't with us for long.

One day I came from the bathroom along the passage to bump into a thick velvet curtain. It had a dark green lining and large tassels and was hanging from a brass rail. Then I saw that the house was mine but furnished differently. The walls were mock panelled up to halfway, above that was wallpaper covered with bright yellow flowers like fallen roses. The carpet was dark green and shone like satin.

I stood in the passage in my working clothes, with the wax polish and yellow duster, staring at the upper landing with my mouth open. A door on the upper landing opened and an elegant young lady of about twenty five came out. Her hair was in Marcelle waves but I think she had a bun. I do a lot of knitting and can describe her dress perfectly. It was knitted in a 4 ply tweed white and green wool. The cardigan was down below the hips, the skirt was knitted in four panels and hung about three inches above her ankles. The belt of her cardigan was hanging as she moved. Her blouse was turquoise, blending with her suit, and was almost see-through. She had cream shoes with funny heels and an ankle strap.

As she came through the door she was whistling through her teeth, but saw me, stopped and looked very flustered. I grinned. She came down the steps towards me, holding the bannisters which were nicely polished, not brown paint as they are to day, and sidled nervously past. As she went by she flipped her heel. Then a second or two later I found myself back in my present house. Could this have been Clarissa Steadman? Marcelle waves were in fashion in about 1915. Then, which one of us was the ghost - did she come into my time or did I go into hers?

What an interesting question this is. This time slip seems much more likely than in other cases. What is more, it seems that the young lady with the Marcelle waves also saw the narrator. If anyone has any record of a young lady who once lived in a house off Tachbrook Road round about 1915 and saw a ghost holding a yellow duster and a can of furniture polish, the publishers would be interested. The mignonette perfume is obviously another psychic aroma.

The Nun, the Priest & the Redcoats (Princethorpe)

The spire of Princethorpe College Church can be seen for many miles. The College was built in 1832 for a group of French nuns who had escaped from the French Revolution and settled at Abbots Salford. The building has had various uses over the years and is now a Catholic boys' school.

There are many rumours in Princethorpe about sightings of ghostly nuns and phantom battles. A group of trees is known as Nun's Wood and beside it is a field with undulations which are said to be the scars of war. Some local people will tell you that phantom battles have been witnessed.

One such sighting was recorded by the Coventry Evening Telegraph of 8 December 1984. In the mid 1950's a local farmer was cycling past the field when he heard shouting and noise. Throwing down his bike he hurried to the hedge to see a nun and a priest fighting off about twenty red coated soldiers. Some of them were brandishing swords, others were searching the edge of the wood. Both the nun and the priest were slashed by the swords, then the scene faded.

A year later the same farmer was walking past the field when a man rushed out in terror. He was a stranger to the area and had parked his car to pick bluebells when he saw the figure of a nun walk past some yards away. He was shocked when she walked straight through a barbed wire fence.

Some months later, the farmer saw a nun walking towards him along the path. He was determined to speak to her and deliberately stood in her way. She walked straight through him, and as she did he felt a tingling sensation.

In the years that followed, the farmer saw the nun at least a dozen times, always at the same time of day and crossing the road towards the trees. On one occasion the figure of a priest or monk emerged from a hedge and crossed the road three yards from him. There was an expression of rigid agony on his face. The farmer has not seen anything for many years. He wonders if the ghosts had appeared to protest at the ground being sold off piece by piece to property developers.

These time slip cases raise all sorts of problems and this one is a classic. On the face of it, the scene which the farmer witnessed could not have happened on that spot at any time. There have been no religious persecutions by the state since the Priory was founded and, if the incident occurred earlier there is the problem of the soldiers' red coats. This uniform came well after the end of religious persecutions. So what did Mr Barlow see? One possible explanation is that he saw something which did happen but somewhere else, a misdelivered image as it were.

Another possibility is a complex hallucination proceeding from his own subconscious and rooted in imagination, forgotten reading, overheard stories or other sources. It seems that glimpses of the future are quite often accurate, but supposed glimpses of the past are often misleading.

The Vanishing Hitch Hiker
(Alcester)

In such a car orientated area as the Midlands it would be surprising if we did not come across that well travelled ghost who is a fundamental part of the folklore of the motor car, the Vanishing Hitch-hiker.

South of Alcester the A435 passes both gates of Ragley Hall, then two miles further on it meets the main road from Redditch at Dunnington Cross Roads, where the old Birmingham turnpike ended through lack of funds.

The following story has been contributed by the Marquess of Hertford. He inherited Ragley Hall at the age of nine and has devoted his life to restoring this magnificent Palladian house where his family have lived since 1680.

"On the A435 halfway between the Ragley Lodge gates and Kingley Corner is a place called The Springs. I think there is still a water trough there. Beside this spring there sometimes stood a little old lady who was apparently in the habit of wanting a lift from any passing carriage to Dunnington cross roads. The driver would get down to assist the old lady out of the carriage, only to find she was not there. After a time, and after complaints were being made that the old lady was alarming people, somebody dug around the spring and found the bones of an old woman. They were laid to rest in Arrow Churchyard in the early years of this century, and the little old lady was never seen again."

Those bones may rest at Arrow, but the Hitch-hiker marches on. There is a road in North Somerset where drivers have been picking up non existent hitch-hikers (male and female) for years. At Bluebell Hill in Kent drivers give lifts to a girl in a blue dress or coat who vanishes from their car. Bluebell Hill was the scene of a fatal accident many years ago, one victim of which was a young lady about to be married. Local legend identifies her as the Kent hitch-hiker.

Nowadays she (or he) rides in motor vehicles, but the Hitch-hiker is far older. William Henderson, in *Folklore of the Northern Counties* (1866, reprinted BP Publishing 1973) quotes a case from the north east in the mid eighteenth century. Farmers returning from market gave lifts to a little old lady who wanted to reach a certain bridge. Always she vanished from the cart before it reached the bridge. Eventually, digging beneath the bridge revealed the bones of a woman who had been murdered. When they were laid to rest the Hitch-hiker was seen no more.

Across America, drivers pick up a young girl and drop her in the country, lending her a coat or scarf against the rain. If they call back for the clothing, someone tells them that their description of the girl matches a daughter who died a year or more before. A visit to the grave finds the coat or scarf there, neatly folded. Even film star Telly Savalas has picked up America's Vanishing Hitch-hiker.

Professor Jan Harold Brunvand of the University of Utah, in *The Vanishing Hitch-hiker; Urban Legends and their Meanings* (Picador 1983) says:

"This returning ghost tale was known by the turn of the century both in the United States and abroad. It acquired the newer automobile motif by the time of the Great Depression, and thereafter spawned a number of sub types with greatly varied and oddly interlocking details, some of which stemmed from earlier folk legends."

He cites dates back to 1876 and places from Moscow to Korea. Rodney Dale, in *The Tumour in the Whale* (Universal Books 1978), cites a version where a fortune teller is given a lift. She tells a driver that before he reaches home there will be a corpse in his car, but this is not all.

"That there will be no war (if the story is told before the war) or that the war will end on a certain date (if the story is told during the war). Other versions foretell Hitler's death, he being the force behind the war. The fortune teller is set down, and the traveller continues on his journey: however, either he takes on another passenger, or he calls at the house of a friend who seeks a lift for himself (or another), or he comes across a road accident and takes the victim to hospital. Whatever the detail, he takes a passenger, and the passenger dies in transit."

In more modern versions, the prophetic hitch-hiker is a nun or a beautiful young hippy clad in white, who prophecies the second coming of Christ before vanishing.

The Vanishing Hitch-hiker is the most famous of all urban legends. Stories and television plays have been woven around her, the pop song *Laurie - Strange Things Happen* derived from her, she appears in Ernest Baughman's *Type and Motif Index of the Folktales of England and North America*, the only modern story to be so honoured. She seems adaptable, indestructible. As long as man travels she will go with him.

Where and when and how did her endless journey begin? She might be an hallucination. Reports are noticeably more frequent among those who drive long distances. She could be a manifestation of road hypnosis, of the driver's subconscious throwing up an archetypical hallucination when his conscious mind has been dulled by long hours gazing at the road.

She might be an optical illusion. In north Hampshire drivers cresting a hill at night see a lady in a red jacket standing by a bus stop. New bus drivers on the local route pull up for her, to the laughter of regular passengers, who know that she is an effect formed by shadows and a post box.

Our guess is that she has more distinguished ancestry. Bran, the God King of the Celts, and Odin of Scandinavia travelled the world in disguise allowing themselves to be picked up by strangers, and she might be either of them. Another ancient being is the Morrigan or the Cailleach, the Hag with Seven Husbands, who met ancient Celtic heroes on their journeys and prophesied the outcome of wars and battles. She dwelt by springs and wells and was worshipped at them.

Were the bones found near Ragley Hall those of an ancient Celtic sacrifice to the Cailleach or one of her priestesses? Is the Vanishing Hitch-hiker so deeply embedded in our subconscious that she will follow us to the stars?

The Phantom Battle (Edgehill)

Eric Hall of Leamington is an ex member of the Sealed Knot Society, whose aim is to perpetuate memories of events in three English civil wars, and from time to time they re-enact battles. Eric's favourite battle in which he took part for many years, is Edgehill. He is so taken with it that he even smokes a clay pipe.

Eric is therefore an authority on Edgehill and its ghosts. His house is full of old books and snippets of information, including newspaper cuttings of ghostly appearances since 1947. He has provided the following information.

Edgehill on 23rd October 1642 was the first great battle of the Civil War between Charles I and the Parliamentarians. Twenty four thousand men fought over a battlefield ten miles south-east of Stratford upon Avon, and many died.

Three months after the battle a London printer published a pamphlet which said, "On Saturday - which was in Christmas time, between 12 and 1 o'clock in the morning", a group of shepherds, some travellers and a few local people, had heard, "first, the sound of drums afar off, and the noise of soldiers, as it were giving out their last groans". The pamphlet tells how they watched the battle re-enacted in the sky for three hours, not daring to run away in case they were caught up in the fighting. When it was over, the spectators hurried to Kineton to tell Mr Wood (the local JP), and his neighbour, Mr Marshall (the Minister).

The next night (the Sunday before Christmas) Mr Wood, Mr Marshall and others went to the battlefield and were amazed to see it repeated. Rumours of it reached the King who sent a Colonel, two Captains and three high ranking gentleman to investigate. They stayed in Kineton until the following Saturday night, when the battle in which they had taken part was again re-enacted and they recognised several of their slain comrades.

The public, including the local people, were as sceptical about the story as they would be today. Then a few days after the first pamphlet a second appeared, describing the apparitions and saying that on 4 January the battle was seen by the local townsfolk who, "being abed were woken when the dolefull and hydious groanes of dying men were heard".

The battle was re-enacted again in the 1860's. Miss R M Seaton, former Matron of Uppingham School, reported that when she was a child an elderly uncle had told her that, as a boy he had gone with a group of newspaper reporters to Edgehill. Several went towards the ridge where the army could be seen on the skyline. All returned shaking and frightened saying that they had heard the clash of weapons.

On 5 January 1947 the *Banbury Advertiser* reported that soldiers stationed at Marlborough Farm Camp, Burton Dassett, regularly met the spectral figure of a white horse while on night duty. This was assumed to be the great white charger of Prince Rupert. Five days later the Birmingham Evening Mail said that the ghost of Prince Rupert's white horse was persistently seen. It was described as "a charger, full of spirit and performance, foaming at the mouth, is seen to clear a hedge then vanish". It was seen by the postman at Tysoe, the Tysoe policeman when on night patrol and a well known resident and lay preacher, Mr G Orme Riley.

The next recorded sighting of the phantom horse was on 24 December 1950, when the Sunday Mercury reported that it had been seen in daylight as well as at night. A Banbury resident had also heard a ghostly chorister singing in the old priest's room behind the alter in Warmington church. In the graveyard lies the body of Alexander Gourdin who died of wounds the day after the battle. Two years later, a couple of stray characters wearing dark hoods and cloaks terrified a baker's boy from Gaydon, floating across his handlebars as he cycled along the Banbury road near the battlefield.

The most likely time for a re-enactment would be during the anniversary of the battle, and Eric has spent many cold nights in the last three months of each year walking round the battlefield. He had to get permission from the military authorities as part of the area was an ammunition depot. Eric spent some time chatting to soldiers waiting to go on duty, and he heard about the incident of December 1976 which was later reported in the Coventry Evening Telegraph.

At 12.50 am one moonless night, Private Haywood (a dog handler) and his dog were patrolling the area when the dog backed off and cowered. They rounded a bend and entered a clearing to see the white, blurred figure of an hunched old man with his head sunk onto his shoulders. It was walking straight across the railway line and Private Haywood challenged it, but it disappeared. Private Haywood said he radioed to base to say he had seen someone, then scarpered.

Eric was rewarded for his patience and perseverence. On the still, bitterly cold night of 31 October 1964, at 5.17 pm Eric and his friend, John Lovell heard hymn singing and beating of drums from the Radway direction. At first they thought it was from a pub, but the nearest was over a mile away at Ratley, and did not open until 6.00 pm.

Tragically, the soldiers of 1642 were not the only ones to lose their lives at Edgehill. In 1957 soldiers and guard dogs on military manoeuvres were killed when their truck was hit by a train near Thistle Farm. Near the scene of the accident is a large galvanised water tank and the soldiers often paused here for their dogs to take a drink. Several soldiers told Eric that twice in 1957, during July and just before Christmas, two soldiers and a dog glowing in a blue haze were seen. In the July, they passed close by the two soldiers on duty who recognised them as their lost friends.

✳

Edgehill is not the only battle said to have been re-enacted, and battle hauntings, like time slips, are problematical. Glib explainers will tell you that one of the causes of hauntings is the energy matrix left behind by people dying suddenly or violently, which can be detected much later by suitably sensitive people. Which sounds very good until you think about the evidence.

Two English ladies on holiday in France some years after World War II slept in a room near one of the D-day invasion beaches. They were kept awake by the sound of battle from the beach. When they described it, experts said that they had described the real progress of the invasion battle on that beach. Now those ladies heard automatic gunfire and artillery and mechanised vehicles. Do tanks leave an energy matrix and have ghosts. Is Edgehill haunted by the ghosts of drums and muskets, as well as horses and men?

A possible explanation of some ghosts is that certain conditions impress upon the landscape a kind of recording of violent events. When a sensitive person of the right kind enters the field of the recording it will replay to them images of what occurred. The idea was used years ago in a play called *The Stone Tape* by Nigel Kneale. It suggested that a combination of local electromagnetic fields and the chemistry of the surroundings might cause the recording. It is an ingenious theory and one that makes more sense of hauntings like Edgehill or the D-Day replay. What is more, there are devices that can detect the pattern of static electricity in the pile of a carpet where a foot has been pressed and left no visible outline, and we have instruments that can detect (and photograph) the thermal images of people who are no longer in a room, and cars no longer parked in a street.

The white horse at Tysoe is curious for a number of reasons. Ghosts of animals are usually bad news, and for Midlanders white horses bring bad luck - unless you spit when you see them. Tysoe has another connection with horses. Until 1798 there was on a hillside a mile south of the Stratford to Banbury road at Tysoe, a figure of a horse cut out of the turf. Said to have been cut in 1461, it was supposed to commemorate the death of the Earl of Warwick's charger at the Battle of Towton on Palm Sunday that year.

However, some have suggested that the figure predates the battle of Towton by a long way. The Tysoe horse was the subject (like its famous brother on the Berkshire Downs) of a scouring ceremony and festivity on Palm Sunday. It led to the area being marked on old maps as the Vale of the Red Horse, for the local earth is red. Horse and festival have vanished and trees cover the site, so the outline of the Red Horse of Tysoe can only be detected by infrared aerial photography.

The Country Boy (Edgehill)

The story of the ghostly Battle of Edgehill is well known, but people have other strange experiences in the area. They are reluctant to make them public and the following two incidents have only come to light because the father of the young man concerned, who lives on the north western edge of the battlefield, persuaded him to tell his story.

"One evening, in 1975, when I was about nine, my father and I went in the car to see friends at Leamington. We decided to return on the back route to Kineton by the old road which used to be gated, so you had to keep stopping and getting out to open the gates. As my father drove along, I suddenly realised that he was about to crash into a young boy sitting on one of the gates which remained across the road. He was about the same age as me and I particularly remember his haircut which was a real, classic, basin cut. His clothes were a dark tweed and he was wearing short trousers and hobnail boots. He had rosy cheeks and was smiling, and with him was a black and white collie dog.

I grabbed the steering wheel and turned the car to avoid him. My father stopped looked at me and said, *"What did you do that for?"* I pointed out that he had nearly hit a boy on the gate. We got out of the car to look and the road was clear - there was no gate, no boy, no dog, nothing.

I saw the boy once more, later that year. Again, I was in the car which my father was driving late at night along the old gated road. This time the boy was sitting on a fence at the side of the road, nonchalantly watching the world go by, still smiling, still with his dog.

I asked round locally and though many people have verified that the road was once gated, no one has any idea as to the identity of the young boy."

The House over the Waters
(Stratford upon Avon)

Not many people realise that the little River Rother flows beneath the main street of Stratford upon Avon, and nearby streets have streams beneath them. The house featured below stands over a confluence of two streams. Some people think that a convergence of water helps to create an energy for psychic phenomena. This is the only explanation which Mrs Hicks* can suggest for the strange occurrences in the house, but says she positively misses the entities who shared her home for ten years.

She moved into the late Regency corner house near the town centre during the late 1950's. It was light and airy with large windows and caught the sun all day. The ghosts didn't seem to be intimidated by the sunshine and a whole company of them continued their hauntings by day and by night.

"The night we moved in, I put my three little girls to bed in a room on the first floor. Suddenly, they all started crying, *"Mummy there's a face at the window"*. I told

them not to be silly and asked them how anyone could be
at the window when it was so high up from the ground.

One of the first oddities was that whenever I was expecting a
visitor, the doorbell would ring a few minutes before they
arrived. I used to go to the door and there would be no one
there. Then a few minutes later the bell would ring again
and the visitor would be standing there. I solved this by
not answering until the bell had rung twice.

Nothing much happened for about twelve months. I lived
on the first and second floors, someone else lived on the
separate ground floor and an enclosed staircase gave me
private access. We began to notice that someone would
come in through the front door, slam it shut and come up the
staircase. The footsteps would pause outside the sitting room
before going up the next staircase to the top landing, but no
one could be seen. This would happen several times a day. I
kept going out and though I could hear the footsteps and the
floorboards creaking, I could see nothing. I used to flatten
myself against the wall to let whatever it was go past.

The family joked about this and called the presence George.
"It" was with us at least three times every day or evening.
The children grew up accepting George's presence, to them it
was normal to have people around that we couldn't see. This
was brought home when my eldest daughter was twelve. I
had left the children for a short while, and as I returned
with a friend through the front door, my daughter came out
of the sitting room and shouted, *"George!"*.

The house was so large it always seemed to need decorating.
I managed most of it but couldn't cope with the stairwell. A
friend of mine said she would decorate it and she brought
trestles, planks and ladders. On the day she started I went
out about 3.00pm to meet my children from school.

When I got back this poor girl was standing by the gate, as
white as her overalls. She had been painting the ceiling
when she heard someone come in, heard the door slam and

footsteps coming up the stairs. She thought it was my eldest daughter and called, *"Lucy, I'm up here"*. The footsteps came on, and at the second staircase she heard a rustling noise and thought it was Lucy carrying something like a big dry cleaners' bag. The she realised that the sounds were very near but she couldn't see anyone. She was terrified.

After that we decided that George was female and renamed him Georgette. I also decided that she was a very benign entity; she never gave you a feeling of discomfort as she walked by, though she always inspected any male visitors, usually in middle of the night.

A male schoolteacher came down to breakfast after his first night and asked, *"Were you walking around at three o'clock this morning? I heard someone"*, he said, *"They came into my room and I could hear them breathing and the curtains rustling."* I said, *"It must have been one of the children"*, because I never admitted to anyone that the house was haunted. They would have thought we were all quite mad.

Another of our guests was Lorraine, a languid young lady. All went well for the first two or three days, then she came down to breakfast very agitated and announced that she wasn't stopping with us. The previous night her fiancee had come to see her. He had a job interview first thing the next morning and Lorraine had promised to lend him her alarm clock, but the clock had been forgotten.

Lorraine went to bed, turned out the lights and was getting comfortable when she heard noises in the room, as if furniture was being moved. Thinking her fiance had come back for the clock she called, *"John, don't make such a noise, you'll wake everyone"*. There was no answer so she turned on the light, but there was nobody there and the furniture was all in place. She turned off the light and the noises started again, so loudly she was quite convinced that it would wake up the whole household. Again she put on the light, but it was as before. She was so frightened that she slept for the rest of the night with the light on. Whatever was causing all the noise, I'm perfectly sure it was not Georgette. She was the only one who was really well behaved. You will gather that Georgette was not the only ghost living with us. We had a number of them. Most people don't seem to realise that ghosts don't take up any space so you can have a dozen, say, living quite happily in one house.

There were many, many, incidents, most of them too trivial to relate, but I remember one evening. I was sitting on the sofa in my sitting room with a friend, the coffee table was in front of us and my King Charles spaniel on the sofa between us. Then the puppy started peering intently across the room, her eye ducked under the coffee table and she scrambled over my lap to look at the floor. She was watching something in the room and you could tell it was an animal because her eyes were fixed at a certain height. Whatever it was, she wasn't upset by it, just curious.

Once when vacuuming I looked down the long corridor and caught a glimpse of a tall man in a long dark coloured overcoat outside the sitting room. I didn't think anything of it and carried on vacuuming, but in the evening a friend came round and we went into the sitting room. I went in first, she followed and started to close the door, but suddenly jerked it back open again. She said, *"I could have sworn there was a man standing outside the door"*. Whoever that was, we never saw him again.

A frequent incident which could be startling was that when we were in the sitting room in the early evening, there would be a tremendous crash from above. It was like somebody holding a heavy object above their head and letting it drop, and it reverberated. This would happen just once. At first we went to see what had fallen but nothing had ever moved. I cleared all furniture from the top landing so when we heard the crash we took no notice, but it did make one jump.

The sitting room adjoined the house next door, and the old lady who lived there was deaf. She used to have her television on so loud that I didn't need the sound on mine. One

(132)

night I was reading, and the noise from next door was so irritating that I got a hammer. In the hallway I hammered, bang, bang, bang, on the adjoining wall, then waited to see if her television would be turned down. It wasn't, but after two or three minutes I heard bang, bang, bang, from another corridor. That really froze me.

One night just before my middle daughter's seventh birthday, she came downstairs to the sitting room sobbing so hard that she couldn't speak, nearly hysterical. I pulled her onto my lap and comforted her until she could tell me there were voices in her bedroom. She said that they were children's voices whispering very, very loudly. *"Who are you? Why are you here? What do you want? Who are you? What are you doing? Who are you?"* I persuaded her to return to bed with the biggest teddy bear to keep her safe, but it wasn't until she was an adult that she told me that she had had to walk through the voices to get out of the bedroom, as they seemed to be round the doorway.

The same thing happened two nights later and I just didn't know what to do. I moved the children into another room and believe it or not, asked Georgette to watch over them. I'm sure that Georgette was a benign influence on the house and she was around daily; I almost felt she was a friend.

Other nights, when the house was quiet at the same time of night, we would hear a child sobbing. It was quite faint, you had to cock one ear to listen, but it was heart breaking. I felt helpless, there was nothing I could do to comfort it. It seemed that we also had another child, a little older, and one would hear her calling. I don't know whether it was Mama or Mummy because it wasn't very clear, but it was a child about four years old. My children decided to leave their toys out for her, and deliberately put things where they thought that she would find them.

Cleaning one day in the attic bedrooms, I had the radio on loud so that I could hear it above the noise of the vacuum. I heard a child calling so I turned off the machine and shouted *"I'm up here"*. It was broad daylight with the sun streaming through two windows. Nobody came upstairs; it was too early for my children to be home from school and I was alone in the house.

We lived opposite a park where I often took the dog for a walk. One evening I was sitting enjoying the warm night air and waiting for the dog to return from a run, when I looked up at our windows. At an attic window I saw the fair curly hair of a young child. She was bending over and straighening up again, as if playing. Calling the dog, I crossed the road and raced up to the attic bedrooms, quite convinced that my youngest daughter was out of bed. When I looked in she was fast asleep and hadn't moved, and I realised that the child in the window had much shorter hair. Under that window my girls had been playing hospitals. A row of shoeboxes against the skirting board each held a little doll. Before going to bed they said they were leaving it for the little girl child to play with it, so I presume that is what she was doing.

Early one evening friends came to see me bringing their little boy of two. We were in the sitting room and the boy was on the sofa eating a biscuit. Then he shuffled along the sofa and patted the seat beside him. He offered his biscuit to somebody invisible saying, *"Bikky"*. A few days later my friend phoned to tell me that her son had taken whoever it was home with him. He told them that it was a little girl with fair hair and her name was Elizabeth. He had been playing with Elizabeth for most of the time since his departure. They were not very pleased. It was some months before Elizabeth faded out of his life.

Every night when I go to bed I read for half an hour or so and when I finish, put my glasses on the bedside table. One morning I reached for them but they weren't there. I peered down at the floor and patted things, I called the children to look, but we couldn't find them. Then we pushed the bed to the other end of the room but still there were no specs. We pushed the bed back and I sat on the edge. Looking down at the floor I saw the glasses between my feet. I didn't know

(134)

whether to laugh or be angry and finally I said out loud (the children had gone) *"I suppose you think that's funny"*, and I'll swear there was laughter in the room.

I discovered that the house had earned a reputation for being haunted over many years. Someone who came to visit my youngest daughter sat down in the sitting room and said, *"Its haunted this house, isn't it?"*. I never told anyone that it was. I just used to answer, *"How do you mean?"*. She told me that she knew someone who used to live here in 1935 and her friend had said it was haunted by a lady in grey.

Another time, an elderly electrician came to fit a storage heater. Over a cup of tea he said, *"Funny house this"*. He told me that he had worked on it for two old ladies in 1917. The police fetched the electricians in the middle of the night because there was a fire in one of the downstairs rooms. It was in the centre but appeared not to have burned anything, not even the floorboards. This happened twice, the second time the fire was in the skirting board in our sitting room. No electricity ran near it and again, the fire had done no damage.

The lady who lived beneath our part of the building was very retiring and we left each other alone. However, after I mentioned that we had had some odd incidents she said, *"That's funny, I've heard heavy breathing in my bedroom."*

For some years if I went out in the evenings I would have a quiet word with Georgette and ask her to keep everything quiet in the house. On a clear and frosty October night a group of friends came to call for me. I had asked a girl of 17 to babysit and with all the chatter and the laughter, I forgot to speak to Georgette, and I do blame myself for this.

When we came back at about 8.30 they left me at the gate and went to find a parking space. The front door was wide open, the lights and TV were on and the fire was burning, but the house was deserted. I ran to the top bedrooms and the children were not in their bunks. I was so bewildered that I patted the bunks in case my eyes were playing tricks. Then a neighbour called me from the front door, *"It's alright, they're all round at our house"*. The girls were wrapped in blankets and sitting in armchairs, the dog and the babysitter were there, and this was the story they told.

The two younger children had gone to bed and my eldest daughter was downstairs with the babysitter. They heard the youngest daughter crying, so Lucy rushed upstairs. The bedroom door had a faulty latch; you could pull it to but it would not actually latch, which meant you could just push it open again. Lucy pushed the door but it was solid. She thought that the youngest was hammering on the other side with her fists. Lucy shouted, *"Get away from the door, I can't open it"*, and suddenly it gave way.

The youngest child was not near the door, she was standing in the middle of the room screaming. Lucy knelt down to put her arms round her and felt as if she was suffocating. The baby-sitter had followed up the stairs. Now she had her hands on the doorposts with something pushing the middle of her back, trying to force her into the room. She started screaming.

While this was going on the middle child was sitting in the top bunk, quite oblivious and reading a book. They called her two or three times and she couldn't think what was wrong, but eventually agreed to follow them. They went down into the street with the younger children in their nightclothes, and round to the neighbour's house. This event took place in the room where my middle daughter had heard the voices.

I was shattered and horrified because nothing frightening had ever happened before. We did not live in fear, we treated these beings with a sense of humour, we gave them names and treated them as a matter of interest and everyday occurrence. We were not even frightened of the dark. I often wandered around with no lights on, not looking for anything, I just liked the dark, and the children were much the same. There is usually nothing to fear from these people. It wasn't until the final incident that everybody was genuinely frightened because it was so inexplicable and it was unlike anything that had happened before. I had to take my eldest daughter to the doctor and she took tranquillisers for a few weeks.

I knew something had to be done so I went to the Parish church, found a priest, and told him what had happened. I said that I didn't want an exorcism, and he suggested that he came round and blessed the house. I don't believe in exorcisms. If there are lost spirits or some entity in a house that is troubled it is no good telling them to go away. They may not know where to go or have nowhere to go.

This man listened to me and believed me and came back to the house. We went to the top floor, which was the noisiest and the most troubled, and he said some prayers. I stood and watched him and listened. He stood there with bowed head for a few minutes then said, *"All will be quiet now"*. With my usual scepticism I said, *"How do you know?"* and he replied *"Because the voice of God told me"*. Afterwards the house was quiet, no more voices, no more sightings, no more noises. We stayed for another two years."

What are Ghosts ?

One thing is certain; no single theory will ever explain all the phenomena that are usually lumped together as ghosts, psychic phenomena, the paranormal etc. The manifestations are too diverse.

Telepathy will explain deathbed apparitions, but it will not explain battlefield images or poltergeists. There may be a single root cause behind many psychic manifestations, in the same way that electricity can be used for electric fires, telephones, TV sets or refrigerators, but the mechanisms of each may be widely different.

Some phenomena may come from within us, others from outside, and some may be triggered in us by external agencies. The magnetic field of the earth is not even; it fluctuates from time to time and place to place. One study has suggested that when the field rises above about one gauss, incidents of spontaneous combustion take place as a response by some human bodies to the increased field.

In Canada, Doctors Michael Persinger and G F Lafreniere collected more than 7000 reports of "anomalous phenomena" covering a period of 160 years. They discovered a tendency for these reports to cluster at twenty year intervals in the same places, with occasional worldwide increases. They related the increases to activity in the earth's magnetic field caused by seismic activity. They wrote of how the human brain can be disturbed to the point of total hallucination by electrical disturbance:

> "The stimulation of the electrically unstable portions of the brain, such as the hippocampal formation, could allow the person access to imagery of epileptic, aura like form. This would be intense and indistinguishable

from reality. Pre event amnesia associated with the electric shock induced alteration in consciousness could allow confabulation characterized by that person's beliefs and fantasies."

In other words, shocked into an apparently real vision, a victim would later have no memory of the shock that caused the hallucination and would try to fit their vision within their own beliefs, whether of fairies, ghosts or little green men from Mars.

Since Persinger and Lafreniere's study, we have learned more about the human brain. Now we know it contains a pattern of tiny permanent magnets. Though we do not yet know their purpose, one thing is clear - they make of each of us a living, moving magnetic pattern within the fluctuating field of the planet on which we live. Do they create an individual "code" by which, perhaps, telepaths can locate each other over any distance? Can they fault in some way that causes spontaneous combustion? Can they be overcharged from within or without to make us hallucinate? Are they the source of an energy matrix that lingers after the death of the body? Can they distinguish such a matrix in their vicinity? Can they charge the subconscious of a teenager with sufficient energy to move large items of furniture, or can they channel that energy from elsewhere?

Not only do we live on a magnetic planet, but it is influenced by outside events. Sunspots can wreak havoc on our radio and television networks, but when they occur their influence flows out for millions of miles beyond the earth. What do they do to our own magnetic structures, far more sensitive than broadcasting systems?

Question after question, and how are they to be answered? By painstaking accumulation of the best reports of psychic phenomena, by analysis and evaluation by experts to reveal common patterns, by the construction of reasonable theories based on those patterns and devising repeatable experiments to prove or disprove them. This has long been the approach of investigators in any field, but too many scientists have been too afraid or too bigoted (or simply not funded) to apply it to the paranormal.

Some patterns are clear. There are many more accounts from women than men. Far more women were burned for witchcraft. Poltergeists more often manifest around girls than boys, more women are mediums, more women seem to die of spontaneous combustion. So are women more gullible, or more psychic? No - it is because of a fundamental difference in the way the two sexes use their brains.

The brain is divided into two halves, the left half governing functions on the right side of the body and vice versa. The two halves of the brain also operate in different modes. The right hand half controls the creative function, intuition and instinct, while the left side deals with logic and analysis. Research has demonstrated that women approach problems and crises through the right side and reach an intuitive solution, while men use the left side to try and think their way through a situation.

Linda Picknett, in *Flights of Fancy* (Ward Lock 1987) questions the effects of this:

> "Is the common link an intense but perverted surge of creativity? Or does the panic implicit in psychological crises cut off the normalizing influence of the left hand brain, laying women open to the chaotic occult forces inside and outside us all, just waiting to pounce? Perhaps there is something in the ancient idea of possession after all."

Ms Picknett, we believe, is wrong. It is not a question of lurking occult forces seizing on vulnerable, non analytical women. It is more probably a question of natural forces acting on the brains of both men and women, and in the case of women, triggering the right hand brain more often, if only because it has had more exercise.

The astonishing power of the mind to create phenomena was demonstrated in Toronto by a group of experimenters who decided to create a ghost. Specialists within the group constructed the details of a character they called "Phillip"; a designer drew him, a novelist outlined his love life and so on. When all members of the group were familiar with his personality and history, they held sittings to contact him. It took some time, but they succeeded. Phillip began to communicate with them by table rapping, and he evinced more than the character they had written for him. Acoustic analysis showed that Phillip's raps were different from those of a person rapping the table. In *Conjuring Up Phillip* (Toronto 1976) Owen and Sparrow describe how Phillip demonstrated poltergeist effects, lifting the table at which they sat and whirling furniture around the room. He became the greatest non entity to be interviewed on a TV chat show, answering questions by rapping the table provided by the studio, and walking the table up steps to the rostrum.

The Phillip experiment speaks volumes about the possibilities of the Ouija board, and shows that complex "paranormal" phenomena can be generated in the brain. One day Phillip may be the most famous person who never was.

Ancient man must have lived largely through the right brain; his life was so harsh and dangerous that he had to act instinctively to survive. Ever since we began to fight back against our environment and to secure a little safety and comfort, that has been changing, and the influence of the left brain has been increasing. That does not make it, as Ms Picknett characterises it, a "normalizing" influence. It may well be that the excessive use of either side is abnormal and unbalancing. Perhaps, when we have learned how we and the world we live in really operate, we may produce a race that utilises the full, extraordinary powers of both halves of the brain, enabling them to live in harmony with each other and the rest of the world.

You, Too, Could have a Ghost

A question frequently put to those who claim to know about ghosts is; "What can I do if the place where I live or work is haunted?" The short answer is grin and bear it or leave, but perhaps we can go further than that.

Some people (there are several in this book) manage to live quite comfortably with their ghosts, regarding them almost as a family pet and giving them names. Others, even when haunting is doing no apparent harm, become frightened or worried and allow themselves to be driven out.

The first important rule is not to worry. Ghosts do no harm. Worrying about and being frightened by them, does.

Some ghosts that appear as glowing shapes, hiss, crackle, whoosh, or just glide silently about, may well be forms of plasmoid, electrically charged air, or ball lightning. They are potentially dangerous. Our grandmothers used to leave front and back doors open during thunderstorms "to let the lightning pass through". If you think that you are in the presence of ball lightning or something similar, stay as far away as possible and open any doors to let it go. Do not worry. Ordinary lightning kills far more people than ball lightning; about one a year in the United Kingdom.

Poltergeists are increasing in Britain. Charles Fort remarked on their prevalence in the nineteenth century, and suggested that since every home from the lower middle class upwards had underpaid, overworked, teenage servants it was not surprising. Now we have abused, stressed and drug addicted children.

Poltergeists can be talked to, and sometimes talk back, albeit offensively at first. If you speak with respect, affection and concern, they will often go away. If you suffer one, try to identify the person at the centre of it and assess their problem. Treat them with extra kindness, which is all that poltergeists seem to seek. Remember Giraldus Cambrensis' observation that they may be noisy and aggressive, but they harm nobody. In fact, it is sometimes possible to get rid of other manifestations by talking to them, explaining that they disturb you, and asking to be left in peace.

Remember too Giraldus' statement that priests could not deal with poltergeists, and never confront a poltergeist with a priest or an exorcist. They will be seen as authority figures and a threat to the poltergeist and become "storm centres". In some modern cases disturbed teenagers have been driven to the edge of insanity by well meant con frontations with priests.

If you see or hear or smell strange things, make sure that they are not real. They emanate just as easily from poor plumbing, heating, ventilating and electrical systems as from the spirit world. Or they may suggest physical illness. Talk to your Doctor who may be able to diagnose some ordinary medical cause.

Check that the effect is not an optical illusion. Many ghosts are. Find out if the premises stand over underground water, a geological fault or a railway line. They can all produce noises, vibrations and optical effects.

If your haunting disturbs you, do not allow anyone to hold seances or Ouija sessions on the premises. The "Phillip" experiment shows the power that can be unleashed and you may make things worse.

Do not let your mind wander while you are in affected premises. The "Ganzfeld State" is a condition set up in paranormal laboratories where the subject is insulated as far as possible from stimuli such as light, sound and touch. This subdues the left brain, which finds no material to analyse, and encourages the right brain to become more active, increasing clairvoyant or telepathic abilities.

Boring repetitive tasks can induce the same effect, opening your right brain to other people's telepathic images. And if it can find no other stimulation, to fantasies and halluc- inations from the memory and the subconscious. If you find yourself slipping into such a state, make an effort to concentrate on something external. Sit where you can see out of a window or see other people. Play a radio; if the radio music lulls you, switch to a speech programme. Surround yourself with interesting pictures that you can look at while carrying out your boring tasks or, if anyone else is around, talk to them.

You may still find that you cannot rid yourself of the idea that something haunts an area. If you are religious, you might try asking your priest to bless the area. Most of the major churches will do this and it frequently works.

If all else fails, you may wish to consider exorcism. It is not a convenient way of getting rid of the household or office ghost. It is a specific ritual for the casting out of demons. If you are not convinced you are dealing with an evil spirit, leave exorcism alone.

The Roman Catholic Church and the Church of England will carry out exorcisms only by permission of a Bishop, and that is reluctantly given. There is the question of whether an evil spirit is involved, and there is the adverse publicity that such ceremonies can attract. There is also a recognised danger in that a cast out demon may possess the officiating priest. The Church of Scotland does not recognise exorcism. Jews and Muslims have very ancient rituals of their own, but they are rarely practised and it is not unknown for them to use the Christian ritual.

Avoid any priest of any faith who is too anxious to carry out an exorcism. Here and there you will find clerics who believe it to be the ultimate challenge of their faith, who will enter the situation in a spirit worthy of Rambo. Apart from being steeped in the sin of pride, such people are a danger to themselves and others.

In September 1974 a young man in Yorkshire announced to a Christian Fellowship meeting that he was possessed by demons. Six "exorcists", including a Church of England clergyman and a Methodist lay preacher worked over him all night, claiming to have cast out forty demons. The distressed victim of their well meant efforts went home to kill his wife with his bare hands, tearing out her eyes and tongue. Do not invoke the assistance of self appointed exorcists or occultists. In another case, two such sought to cast out demons from a young woman. They became so enthusiatic that they jumped on her as she lay on the floor and crushed her to death.

In the United States there have been cases where parents killed young children in their efforts to drive out devils. Misconceived exorcism is a far greater danger than any paranormal effect.

The ultimate enemy is fear. Try not to be frightened of whatever haunts you and to remember that it will not, cannot, do you any physical harm. Nor can it do you any psychological harm if you are not afraid of it. If you are religious, remind yourself that the most powerful weapon in the Devil's armoury is fear.

Finally, if you cannot accept or ignore your ghost, if it disturbs or worries you and you cannot get rid of it, then it may be time to leave the job or the house. There is no point in living or working in a place that makes you uneasy.

A last cautionary story. Demetrious Myiciura lived in Stoke on Trent and believed that he was pursued by vampires. Heaven knows why - vampires are not reported in the Potteries, and are virtually absent from British supernatural lore. But so worried was he that he adopted every defence. He sprinkled his bed with salt and hung garlic over it; a bowl of garlic and urine prevented vampires getting in through the window. When Myiciura was found dead in 1973 an astute Police officer recognised the anti-vampire precautions, but could not see what had killed him. Post mortem examination proved that he choked to death on a clove of garlic which he had placed in his mouth as an additional precaution.

Bibliography

Brunvand Professor Jan Harold *The Vanishing Hitch-Hiker; Urban Legends and their Meanings*, Picador 1983.

Curtis R H *A Short History of Alvechurch*. Recently published by Alvechurch Historical Society and Alvechurch Village Society

Dale Rodney *The Tumour in the Whale*, Universal Books 1978.

Dent Robert *Old & New Birmingham*, Houghton & Hammond 188C

Giraldus Cambrensis *The Journey through Wales* (1188), translated L Thorpe, Penguin 1978.

Green Andrew *Phantom Ladies*, Bailey Bros & Sinfen Ltd, 1977.

Grice Frederick *Folk Tales of the West Midlands*, Thomas Nelson & Sons, 1952.

Gwinnett Arthur *A History of Alcester*. Published privately 1947.

Gwinnett Aubrey *The Story of the Angel Inn*. Published privately 1966.

Hackwood F W *Staffordshire Customs, Superstitions and Folklore*, E P Publishing, 1974

Prince Rosalind *Some Ghosts of Staffordshire*, Staffordshire County Council.

(And other books, details of which are given in the text).